THE HEGEMONY OF ENGLISH

DONALDO MACEDO

BESSIE DENDRINOS

PANAYOTA GOUNARI

Para

Samantha

y

Sabrina

con

la amistad

de

Dnobб

PARADIGM PUBLISHERS
Boulder Colorado

Published in the United States by Paradigm Publishers, 3360 Mitchell Lane Suite E, Boulder, CO 80301 USA.

Paradigm Publishers is the trade name of Birkenkamp & Company, LLC, Dean Birkenkamp, President and Publisher.

ISBN 978-1-59451-000-7 (hardcover)
ISBN 978-1-59451-001-4 (paperback)

Printed and bound in the United States of America on acid-free paper that meets the standards of the American National Standard for Permanence of Paper for Printed Library Materials.

Designed and typeset by Straight Creek Bookmakers.

10 09   4 5

✢

To all the people who experience subordination in speaking an imposed dominant language yet courageously struggle to sever the yoke of linguistic oppression

CONTENTS

v

INTRODUCTION

⊕

DURING A SYMPOSIUM SOME YEARS AGO ON BILINGUALISM AT THE Harvard Graduate School of Education, a student asked the panelists how they would reconcile their strong support for bilingual education in the United States with the current hegemony of English that was shaping the debate as to how to best educate millions of non-English-speaking students enrolled in the nation's public schools. Before the panelists could address the question, a senior Graduate School faculty member, who is also a language specialist, unabashedly asked, "What is hegemony?" This seemingly naïve (but not innocent) question was followed by a brief silence of disbelief that a senior School of Education faculty member would not know the meaning of hegemony. On closer analysis, one should not be at all surprised that a Harvard language specialist would not understand the concept of hegemony, given the almost total absence of courses in the required curriculum that would expose students to the body of literature dealing with the nature of ideology, language politics, and ethics. Such literature would provide students of language and language education with the necessary understanding and critical tools to make linkages between self-contained technical studies of language and the social and political realities within which this technical approach to language studies often takes place. Graduate students in language education, in particular, and in linguistics, in general, are usually required to take multiple courses in research methodologies (mostly quantitative). However, no such requirements exist, for example, for a course on the nature of ideology, which would help students begin to understand the very ideology that shapes and maintains their often disarticulated approach to language analysis. This very selection process, which prioritizes certain bodies of knowledge while discouraging or suffocating other discourses, is linked to something beyond education: ideology. Thus, the very curriculum selection and organization in language studies favor a disarticulated technical training in preference to courses in critical theory, which would enable students to make linkages with, for example, the status and prestige accorded to certain dominant languages (the languages of the colonizers) and the demonization and devaluation of the so-called uncommon or minority languages (the languages of the colonized).

This curriculum points to the very ideology that attempts to deny its own existence through a false claim of neutrality in scientific pursuits in language studies. The curriculum selection and organization give rise to a social construction of "not naming," thus enabling even highly instructed individuals (i.e. a senior Harvard professor) to feel comfortable, and sometimes arrogantly proud, in dismissing any body of knowledge that falls beyond their narrow and often reductionistic specialized area of study. This arrogance was abundantly clear when this same Harvard Graduate School of Education faculty member admonished a doctoral student for quoting Antonio Gramsci during a graduate seminar presentation by telling him, "It is bad pedagogy to drop names of esoteric authors that one accidentally stumbles upon."

The flippant dismissal of Gramsci's leading ideas with respect to hegemony, in particular, and to language, in general, demonstrates that most educators, particularly in the United States, have blindly embraced a positivistic mode of inquiry which enables them to deny outright the role of ideology in their work. In the process, they try to prevent the development of any counter-discourse within their institutions—as clearly demonstrated by the attempted elimination of Gramsci's ideas at the Harvard Graduate School of Education. The over-celebration of methodological rigor and the incessant call for objectivity and neutrality support their false claim of a scientific posture through which "they may try to 'hide' in what [they] regard as the neutrality of scientific pursuits, indifferent to how [their] findings are used, even uninterested in considering for whom or for what interest [they] are working."[1] Because most language educators and sociolinguists do not really conduct research in the "hard sciences," they disingenuously attempt to adopt the "neutrality" posture in their work in the social sciences, leaving out the necessary built-in self-criticism, skepticism, and rigor of the hard sciences. In fact, science cannot evolve without a healthy dose of self-criticism, skepticism, and contestation. However, a discourse of critique based, for instance, on the ideological understanding of the asymmetrical power relation between dominant and subordinate (euphemistically called uncommon or minority) languages is often viewed as contaminating "objectivity" in language studies and language education. For example, by pretending to treat sociolinguistics as hard science, the sociolinguist "scientist" is often forced to either dismiss factors tied to ideology or to make the inherently political nature of language analysis and language education invisible. In fact, even when sociolinguists, particularly in the United States, describe the relationship between language functions and class (see, for example, the work of William Labov), their analyses never go beyond a mere description of class position and its correlate linguistic functions. In their view, doing a rigorous class analysis that would call for a Marxist framework would be to exit science. It is important to note that there are a handful of sociolinguists and language specialists whose work embraces important questions of ideology, class, race, gender, and the intersection of these factors with the very language under study, such as Basil Berrnstein, James Donald, Pierre Bourdieu, Norman Fairclough, Allastair Pennycook, Robert Phillipson, and Tove Skutnabb-Kangas, among others, all of whom conduct their work outside the United States. It would be safe to assume that, by and large in the United States, most sociolinguists fall prey to the positivistic dogma that generally imposes a disarticulation between science and the ideological and political reality that constructs science, particularly social science, in the first place. One could argue with some level of comfort that by acquiescing to the pressure of positivism, most sociolinguists and language educators unknowingly planted the seeds that have rendered the field of sociolinguistics moribund, particularly in the United States. The promising work of William Labov and many of his contemporaries became truncated by their inability to incorporate fully into their analyses an ideological framework that could have unveiled important insights—for instance, on the relationship between racism and language policy as elegantly suggested by Bessie Dendrinos in her essay here on "linguoracism." The fear of incorporating factors such as race, class, culture, ethnicity, gender, and their intersection with language has enabled most sociolinguists and language educators to treat their analysis of language as if social beings are not participants in the social construction of the very language under study and its respective functions in society. Often, in their zeal for neutrality and impartiality, many sociolinguists and language educators approach the "real world, where the language under study is spoken, as if [they] were wearing 'gloves and masks' in order not to be contaminated by it."[2]

4

These metaphorical "gloves and masks" represent, in our view, an ideological fog that enables these language educators and sociolinguists to comfortably fragment bodies of knowledge. By reducing language analysis to pure technicism, they can more easily disarticulate a particular form of knowledge from other bodies of knowledge, thus preventing the interrelation of information necessary to gain a more critical reading of the complex nexus between language, culture, ideology, class, race, ethnicity, and gender. The urgent need to be viewed as doing "real" science, for example, pushed the important and promising earlier work of William Labov toward the framework of variable rules—an approach that appeared to be more scientific, but which relegated important concepts such as "status" and "solidarity" to the margins of his sociolinguistic analyses. As a result, Labov failed to realize that "status" and "solidarity"—as determinants in language use and function, and as concepts—could not exist outside the ideological reality that gives rise to these concepts in the first place. Even the bilingual movement that developed during the seventies in the United States as a reaction against the rampant mis-education of millions of immigrant children could not escape the positivistic zeal that permeates all language education programs. By its very nature and historical circumstances, the bilingual movement in the United States should have adopted a radical and critical posture. Instead, it was quickly taken over by "experts" who over-emphasized a facile empiricism in their research, and this, in turn, influenced program development based on testing and quantification of English-language acquisition. They also blocked any and all attempts to link bilingual research and programs with questions of racism, class, and other ideological factors that work systematically to devalue students' language and culture. Since the attack launched on bilingual education by conservative ideologues is political and ideological in nature, the bilingual movement, by its early refusal to engage ideology as a central focus for its work, has been unable to fend off the recent backlash. One result has been that referenda to outlaw bilingual education programs in California, Arizona, and Massachusetts were easily approved. The referendum in Massachusetts not only outlawed bilingual education but it also criminalized the teaching of content area in a language other than English. Teachers who violate this newly promulgated anti-bilingual law can be fired, as they can also be sued by parents. The racism inherent in the Massachusetts anti-bilingual referendum becomes blatantly obvious when bilingual education, which serves mostly subordinate immigrant students, is juxtaposed with foreign language education that serves largely white middle-class students who are tracked for college preparation. For example, a bilingual teacher in a Boston school can be fired if caught teaching her students in Spanish while, down the hall, a teacher of Spanish as a foreign language is rewarded for teaching her English-speaking students in Spanish only. The insidious racism demonstrated by the 70 percent of Massachusetts voters (mostly white) who voted to prohibit bilingual education also unveiled the fault line of a fragile democracy—one that allows Ron Unz, a multimillionaire, to bankroll referenda designed to make education policy for linguistic minority individuals whose status as immigrants prevents them from voting. Given the heightened racism and xenophobia in the United States at the present time, it would not be too far-fetched for another white racist multimillionaire in a state like Mississippi to sponsor a referendum once again relegating African-Americans to the back of the bus.

By blindly embracing a model of language education that emphasizes technicism while dismissing and discouraging any critical and radical transformation of education for subordinate-language students, most bilingual education leaders have allowed themselves to remain captives of a colonial education ideology that gives primacy to positivistic and instrumental approaches to literacy concerned mainly with the mechanical acquisition of

English-language skills. A brief analysis of conference programs of the National Association of Bilingual Education (NABE) over the past ten years attests to the almost embarrassing lack of speakers (particularly keynote speakers) whose work includes a critical analysis of the social and political order that created the need for the bilingual movement in the first place. With the exception of a few speakers such as Jim Cummins, the NABE conference presentations in the ten years analyzed were stripped of any sociopolitical dimensions, while they functioned, sometimes unknowingly, to reproduce dominant educational values and meanings. The domestication of most bilingual leaders and educators became abundantly evident during the last annual conference, which took place in Philadelphia in March 2002. The conference shared space with the Federal Office of English Language Acquisition (OELA), which was known until this year as OBEMLA (Office of Bilingual Education and Minority Language Affairs), yet no perceivable protest to this significant name change took place. The change is not merely a function of nomenclature but rather signals a substantive shift that points to the conservative ideology of the Bush administration. The Bush administration erased any mention of bilingual education or minority languages from the agency's name without any public input or debate. Yet the NABE leadership, at least publicly, remained silent during the entire conference concerning this drastic government policy change that affects the education of millions of linguistic minority students. The same level of domestication was evident among the Congressional Hispanic Caucus, "once a stalwart ally of Title VII, when not one of its members voted against the legislation that transformed the Bilingual Education Act into the English Acquisition Act."[3] Most bilingual educators and leaders have been unwilling to embrace a radical posture regarding the undemocratic education of linguistic minority students, and they have rejected the critical tools needed to defend against the onslaught of attacks on bilingual education. As a result, they have been, sadly, relegated to the status of low-level state functionaries whose major task (albeit unknowingly) is to reproduce the very status quo they had earlier purported to oppose.

Against a landscape that celebrates empiricism and methodological elegance over the crucial understanding of the social construction of these concepts in the first place, our present book, *The Hegemony of English,* attempts to challenge the straightjacket fashion with which most language educators and sociolinguists have approached the enterprise of language analysis and its relation to society. We also hope to demonstrate that no language analysis can escape a detour through an ideological framework no matter how many "gloves and masks" it attempts to wear. Most importantly, by making the political and ideological central to our analysis, we not only avoid embracing a social construction of "not naming" it, but we also unmask the dominant discourse in language analysis that attempts to treat language as neutral and autonomous.

In the European Union, English is fast becoming the de facto official language of exchange and communication, and in the United States, similar hegemonic forces are working overtime to outlaw bilingual education under the pretext that learning English only is a benefit. Slogans such as "English for all children" abound, creating the false notion that bilingual education is an obstacle to English-language acquisition. While research in language acquisition has amply demonstrated the social and cognitive advantages of bilingualism, policy makers and conservative educators either arrogantly dismiss the empirical evidence supporting bilingual education, or they manipulate the available data to fit their own ideological end of eradicating bilingual education. Their arguments are sometimes so vacuous as to border on the ridiculous. Take for instance the conservative treatment of the term "bilingual." Whereas in most people's minds bilingualism means the ability to speak two languages, conservatives in the United States use the term to mean education in a language other than English. For instance, a principal in a Massachusetts public school summoned the director of the school's bilingual education program for help with translation because he had a bilingual student in the office that he could not understand. When the bilingual director asked the principal in which languages was the student bilingual, he promptly responded: Spanish. Thus, "bilingual" is used by the dominant hegemonic forces not to mean the ability to speak two languages, but rather to typecast ethnicity as a form of devaluation. When an American speaks two or more languages, he or she is normally not labeled bilingual. In most cases, an American speaking two or more languages would be characterized as a polyglot. In the American case, the ability to speak two or more languages would be viewed as advantageous unless the person who speaks the languages is a subordinate speaker (usually an immigrant), in which case it would be considered a handicap to the learning of English. Even the empty slogan "English for all children" is disingenuous in that it never tells those most affected by the proposition what the cost will be. The cost is generally the abandonment of the student's native language and culture. Thus, the present debate over bilingual education versus education in English only is often misguided to a degree that is almost ridiculous, as evidenced, for instance, by research to prove whether Spanish, is or is not an effective language of instruction. The entire question ignores the fact that the Spanish language has produced a vast literature over centuries which included such universal literary characters as Don Quixote, El Picaro, Don Juan, and La Celestina, among others. Over the past few decades, many Spanish writers have received the Nobel Prize in literature. The issue then could not be the suitability of Spanish as a language of instruction. The real issue is the power of the dominant society to manipulate the debate over the language of instruction as a means to deny effective education to millions of immigrant children in their native languages. It is the same manipulation that creates racist labels such as "limited-English-proficiency students" or "non-English speakers" to identify students whose mother tongue is not English. The same ideology that uses these labels to typecast immigrant students would never refer to Americans learning Greek, for instance, as "limited-Greek-proficiency students" or "non-Greek speakers." On the contrary, if any label were used, it would necessarily conjure a positive attribute, such as "student of Greek," or an "American student learning Greek," or, even better, a "Classics major." Unfortunately, the racism is not restricted to the way subordinate language students are labeled. The field of English as a second language (ESL) also exhibits racism in the markedly white ESL teacher population which serves a markedly nonwhite student population. If one attends the annual conference of Teachers of English to Speakers of Other Languages (TESOL), one will find oneself in a sea of whiteness sprinkled with islets of non-white teachers of English as a foreign language (EFL), given the international nature of the conference. If one moves to conferences in the United States sponsored by state ESL organizations, the islets are almost totally submerged by the all-white composition of the ESL field. In view of the lack of criticism in most ESL teacher training programs, due to their emphasis on the technical acquisition of English, most ESL teachers, even those with good intentions, fall prey to a paternalistic zeal to save their students from "non-English-speaker" status. They seldom realize their role in the promotion and expansion of English imperialism and racist policies—such as the referendum passed in Massachusetts that practically forbids instruction in a language other than English—which are designed to atrophy other languages and cultures.

What the labels to typecast linguistic minority students show is that for most subordinate speakers, bilingualism is not about the ability to speak two languages. There is a radical difference between a dominant speaker learning a second language and a subordinate speaker acquiring the dominant language as a second language. Whereas the former involves the addition of a second language to one's linguistic repertoire, the latter usually inflicts upon the subordinate speaker the experience of subordination when speaking his or her devalued language and the dominant language she or he has learned, often under coercive conditions. Linguistic racism abounds even in the so-called democratic societies, which are marked by asymmetries of power relations along the lines of language, race, ethnicity, and class. Take the case of a highly celebrated marriage contract experiment proposed by the Harvard-trained psychologist, Robert Epstein, who is also editor-in-chief of the magazine *Psychology Today*. His experiment, which was covered by major newspapers in the United States, was premised on the theory that love is a learned behavior. He hypothesized that by narrowing down shared values and by making a commitment to learn to love each other, it would be possible to fall in love. As over 300 letters were sent to him for a possible match, his agent in New York proudly announced that he had rejected "one applicant because she had a foreign accent."[4] Thus, for the Harvard-educated Epstein, a foreign accent was an indication of nonsuitability for marriage to someone who is a native speaker of English. This is an example par excellence of how our society treats different forms of bilingualism. This attitude is also reflected in our tolerance toward certain types of bilingualism and lack of tolerance toward others. Most of us have tolerated various degrees of bilingualism on the part of foreign language teachers and professors, ranging from speaking the foreign language they teach with a heavy American accent to serious deficiency in the mastery of the language they teach. Nevertheless, these teachers, with rare exceptions, have been granted tenure, have been promoted within their institutions, and, in some cases, have become "experts" and "spokespersons" for various cultural and linguistic groups in their communities.

On the other hand, when bilingual teachers are speakers of a subordinated language who speak English as a second language with an accent, the same level of tolerance is not accorded to them. Take the case of Westfield, Massachusetts, where "about 400 people ... signed a petition asking state and local officials to ban the hiring of any elementary teacher who speaks English with an accent," because, according to the petitioners, "accents are catching."[5] The petition was in response to the hiring of a Puerto Rican teacher assigned to teach in the system. A similar occurrence took place some years ago at the prestigious Massachusetts Institute of Technology. A group of students petitioned the administration not to hire professors who spoke English with a foreign accent, under the pretext that they had difficulty understanding their lectures. By barring professors who spoke English with a foreign accent from teaching, these students would have kept Albert Einstein from teaching in U.S. universities. In fact, the Westfield principal lent support to the parents who had petitioned to prevent the hiring of the Puerto Rican teacher by stating that he would not even hire Albert Einstein to teach in his school because Einstein spoke English with a foreign accent. Thus, Einstein's genius as a physicist would be less important for this principal than speaking English without a foreign accent.

Any language debate that neglects to investigate fully this linguistic racism and treats bilingualism as mere communication in two languages, invariably ends up reproducing those ideological elements characteristic of the communication between the colonizer and the colonized. That is, the imposition of English in commercial or political exchanges, whether due to its assumed international status or to the coercive educational policies in English-speaking countries where English is viewed as an education in itself, points to a form of neocolonialism that is characterized by the erasure of "otherness." In this book, we argue that the questions surrounding the prominence of English in commerce and politics in the contemporary world and the imposition of English upon millions of subordinate speakers of other languages who immigrate to English-speaking countries have nothing to do with whether English is a more suitable language for international communication or whether it is a more viable language of instruction in schools. This position would point to an assumption that English is, in fact, a superior language and that we live in a classless, race-blind world. We propose instead that understanding the present attempt to champion English in world affairs cannot be reduced simply to issues of language, but rests on a full comprehension of the ideological elements that generate and sustain linguistic, cultural, and racial discrimination. These elements represent, in our view, vestiges of a colonial legacy in the so-called democracies of the world.

In this book we contend that subordinate languages have to be understood within the theoretical framework that generates them. Put another way, the ultimate meaning and value of subordinate languages is not to be found by determining how systematic and rule-governed they are. We know that already. The real meaning of a language has to be understood through the assumptions that govern it and the social, political, and ideological relations to which it points. Generally speaking, the issue of effectiveness and validity often hides the true role of language in the maintenance of the values and interests of the dominant class. In other words, the issue of the effectiveness and validity of a subordinate language becomes a mask that obfuscates questions about the social, political, and ideological order within which the subordinate language exists.

In this sense, a subordinate language is the only means by which subordinate speakers can develop their own voice, a prerequisite to the development of a positive sense of self-worth. As Henry Giroux elegantly states, voice "is the discursive means to make themselves 'heard' and to define themselves as active authors of their worlds."[6] The authorship of one's own world implies the use of one's own language and relates to what Mikhail

Bakhtin describes as "retelling the story in one's own words."[7]
Telling a "story in one's own words" not only represents a
threat to those conservative educators and political pundits who
are complicit with the dominant ideology, it also prevents them
from concealing, according to Vaclav Havel, "their true position
and their inglorious modus vivendi, both from the world and
from themselves."[8]

In *The Hegemony of English* we also point out that the purpose of English language education in the contemporary world
order cannot be viewed as simply the development of skills aimed
at acquiring the dominant English language. This view sustains
an ideology that systematically disconfirms rather than makes
meaningful the cultural experiences of the subordinate linguistic
groups who are, by and large, the objects of language policies.
For the role of English to become understood, it has to be
situated within a theory of cultural production and viewed as an
integral part of the way in which people produce, transform, and
reproduce meaning. Thus, the role of English must be seen as a
medium that constitutes and affirms the historical and existential
moments of lived experience which produce a subordinate or a
lived culture. It is an eminently political phenomenon, and it
must be analyzed in the context of a theory of power relations
and with an understanding of social and cultural reproduction
and production. By "cultural reproduction" we refer to collective experiences that function in the interest of the dominant
class, rather than in the interest of the oppressed groups that are
the object of dominant policies. We use "cultural production"
to refer to specific groups of people producing, mediating, and
confirming the common ideological elements that emerge from
and reaffirm their daily lived experiences. In this case, such experiences are rooted in the interests of individual and collective
self-determination.

This theoretical posture underlies our examination of how
the present neoliberal ideology in the guise of globalization has

promoted language policies aimed at stamping out the greater
use of national and subordinate languages in the European Union,
international commerce, and schooling within the English-speaking countries. These policies are consonant with a colonial legacy that had as its major tenet the total deculturation of colonized
peoples. Take, for instance, the educational policies of colonization in Africa, where schools functioned as sites to de-Africanize
the natives. As Paulo Freire succinctly wrote, colonial education

> was discriminatory, mediocre, and based on verbalism. It could
> not contribute anything to national reconstruction because it
> was not constituted for [that] purpose. . . . Schooling was
> antidemocratic in its methods, in its content, and in its objec-
> tives. Divorced from the reality of the country, it was, for this
> very reason, a school for a minority and thus against the
> majority.[9]

Colonial schools functioned as political sites in which class,
gender, and racial inequities were both produced and reproduced. In essence, the colonial educational structure seemed
designed to inculcate the African natives with myths and beliefs
that denied and belittled their lived experiences, history, culture,
and language. The schools were seen as purifying fountains where
Africans could be saved from their deep-rooted ignorance, their
"savage" culture, and their primitive language. According to
Freire, the schools served to "reproduce in children and youth
the profile that the colonial ideology itself had created for them,
namely that of inferior beings, lacking in all ability."[10] In many
respects, the policies of globalization and neoliberalism (which
are not so transparent and therefore more insidious) constitute
a re-articulation of a colonial worldview designed to deculturate
so-called Third-World people so that they can be acculturated
into a predefined colonial model. Like the colonial policies of
the past, the neoliberal ideology, with globalization as its hall-

mark, continues to promote language policies which package English as a "super" language that is not only harmless, but should be acquired by all societies that aspire to competitiveness in the globalized world economic order. As a result, many countries, including many developed nations, eagerly promote an unproblematized English education campaign, where those citizens who opt not to learn English become responsible for their own lack of advancement. In other words, English is now associated with success to such an extent that the acquisition of English is deemed necessary for meeting the requirements of our ever more complex technological society. This view is not only characteristic of the advanced industrialized countries of the West; even within Third World countries the development of English has been championed as a vehicle for economic betterment, access to jobs, and increased productivity. Yet in contradiction to this assumption, many former colonial countries that made English their official language because they viewed it as more suited to the pragmatic requirements of capital, have sadly shown little economic advancement. Their policy often produced additional disastrous consequences, the development of national languages, culture, and identity nearly disappeared under the imperatives of economic and technical development.

The association of English with success is also misleading. For example, the fact that approximately 30 million African-Americans speak English as their mother tongue did not prevent the vast majority of them from being relegated to ghetto existence, economic deprivation and, in some cases, to the status of subhumans. It is most naïve to think that the uncritical acquisition of English will always be a great benefit. What is often left unexamined, even within the academy, is how the learning of English, a dominant language, imposes upon the subordinate speakers a feeling of subordination, as their life experience, history, and language are ignored, if not sacrificed. One can safely argue that English today represents a tool, par excellence, for cultural invasion, with its monopoly of the internet, international commerce, the dissemination of the celluloid culture, and its role in the Disneyfication of world cultures.

It is important to highlight the point that language educators and most sociolinguists have been so deeply ingrained in a positivistic method of inquiry that they have, sometimes unknowingly, reproduced the dominant ideological elements that ignore the asymmetry of power relations as mediated by language, especially issues of language and race, and language and gender, and how the interaction of these factors molds particular identities. In their blind embrace of linguistic neutrality, most language educators and sociolinguists allow their programs to be plagued by the constant debate over scientific rigor and methodological refinements, a debate that often hides language issues of a more serious nature. Hence, it makes sense that language specialists and educators are discouraged from linking linguistic supremacy with cultural hegemony, and this keeps other issues of dominance and subordination hidden. As Antonio Gramsci so accurately explained, "[E]ach time that in one way or another, the question of language comes to the fore, that signifies that a series of other problems is about to emerge: the formation and enlarging of the ruling class, the necessity to establish more 'intimate' and sure relations between the ruling groups and the popular masses, that is, the reorganization of cultural hegemony."[11]

Coupled with the obsession with a false neutrality of language, the fact that most language teaching programs, particularly foreign languages (at least in the United States), exist within literature departments that, more often than not, function as pillars of the empire makes even more remote the possibility of raising issues of a more serious nature, such as the role of language in the reproduction of racism. Although there have been strong movements to develop a more interdisciplinary approach in some literature departments, especially in Europe, where cultural studies and language studies, including language pedagogy, are gaining ground and are more and more represented in the curriculum, most literature departments continue to fragment bodies of knowledge and promote the false notion of art for art's sake, making it abundantly easier to disarticulate their enterprise from any political and social concerns. Furthermore, linking literary analysis with social and political concerns is often viewed as distracting the reader from the affective connection with literature as art that provides the reader with avenues to self-fulfillment and, possibly, a joyful experience, the process through which the reading of literature becomes "the intimate reliving of fresh views of personality and life implicit in the work of literature; the pleasure and release of tensions that may flow from such an experience ... the deepening and broadening of sensitivity to the sensuous quality and emotional impact of day-to-day living."[12] However, "the sensuous quality and emotional impact of day-to-day living" seldom refers to any political and ideological analyses of the human misery and oppressive conditions generated by the society within which the literature as art for art's sake is situated. The art-for-art's-sake approach to literary studies still predominates in most literature departments, which discourage any form of linkage between literature and social and political concerns. This is abundantly clear in the work of John Willett, a scholar and translator of Bertolt Brecht. When he evaluated Brecht's artistic contribution, he noted, "The Brecht of [the early period] ... was unlike the 'ruthless cynic of The Threepenny Opera or the Marxist of later years.' Instead he was ebullient, enjoying words for their own sake, caring little for other people's feelings or interests and less still for social or humanitarian causes."[13] This implies that art which shows concern for human suffering by denouncing the unjust social and political (dis)order invariably suffers artistically. It also implies that Marxism automatically disallows any possibility for artistic achievement. What is important to note is that literature as art for art's sake not only fails to make problematic the "emotional impact of day-to-day living" with respect to class conflict, gender, or racial inequalities, but it also provides a refuge for those artists who pretend to remain neutral with respect to social injustices and other social ills. For example, Leni Riefenstahl, who was the cornerstone of Hitler's propaganda machine, continues to deny that her cinematography played any role in advancing the Nazi cause, claiming that she was interested only in beauty and was not "interested in politics at all."[14] While she claims that she saw Hitler as an important person "who was able to offer work to six million unemployed,"[15] her insistence upon disarticulating her art from the Nazi cause and atrocities enables her to disavow any responsibility that the employment of six million Germans came at the cost of six million Jews who were gassed in concentration camps by the very Nazi cause she so artistically promoted through her films.

Furthermore, this approach to literature completely ignores the cultural capital of subordinate groups and assumes that all people have the same access to literature and the language that sustains it. Yet it simultaneously devalues the language and culture of these same subordinate groups. The failure to address questions of cultural capital or structural inequalities means that literature departments tend to reproduce the cultural capital of the dominant class to which the reading of literature is intimately tied. It is presumptuous and naïve to expect subordinate people, who are confronted and victimized by myriad disadvantages and oppressive conditions, to find joy and self-affirmation through the reading of literature alone. Even more important is the failure of literature departments within which most language programs still exist to place adequate value upon language analysis and language education (see chapter 2 for a more detailed analysis of foreign language education). Traditionally, literature departments have seen the study of language only as a doorway to literature and not as an object of knowledge itself. The asymmetrical power relations between literature and language studies reproduce the false notion that anyone trained in literature is automatically endowed (through osmosis) with the necessary skills to teach the language in which the literature is written. This position precludes viewing language teaching as a complex field of study which demands rigorous understanding of theories of language acquisition coupled with a thorough knowledge of the language being taught and its functions in the society that generates and sustains it. The power asymmetry between language education (in some cases including linguistics if it is housed within the literature department) and, let's say, medieval literature, is reflected in the fact that the teacher of the latter is assumed to be qualified to teach language without any specialized training or understanding of the complex nature of language development, while the opposite is never tolerated. That is, a language specialist would be never allowed to teach a course in medieval literature without first acquiring demonstrable background knowledge in medieval studies.

Conservative ideology generally predominates in literature studies (although there are some exceptions where critical theory has opened up the rigid disciplinary boundaries of literary studies, particularly in Europe), and language studies are still, in many ways, controlled by this conservative ideology to the extent that many language programs remain housed within literature departments. It is therefore not surprising that we produce language specialists at the highest level of the academy who do not know the meaning of hegemony and thus do not understand even their own complicity with ideological forces that use language to achieve "the reorganization of cultural hegemony." The convergence of the conservative ideology of most literature departments with the misguided influence of positivism in language studies, including pedagogy, has created a fertile terrain for the continued disarticulation of the technical approach to language analysis from the sociopolitical factors that shape and maintain the fragmentation of bodies of knowledge. This process inevitably prevents the development of a global comprehension of reality within which language studies are inserted. The insidious nature of the fragmentation of bodies of knowledge, which often parades under the rubric of specialization, lies in its inability to reveal how language and culture embody ideological processes, contradictions, and interests, and how these, in turn, influence social practices and language use. What better way to support the pernicious hegemonic forces that are shaping and maintaining the present social world (dis)order than to reward commissars like the Harvard language specialist for not only not knowing the meaning of hegemony, but also for arrogantly admonishing students who turn to Gramsci's illuminating ideas in order to understand and expose the inherent racism in the facile and cynical promotion of English as the language of progress and the savior of civilization.

DONALDO MACEDO
University of Massachusetts, Boston
BESSIE DENDRINOS
National and Kapodistrian University of Athens, Greece
PANAYOTA GOUNARI
University of Massachusetts, Boston

I
THE POLITICS OF INTOLERANCE:
U.S. LANGUAGE POLICY IN PROCESS

֍

THE UNITED STATES HAS HAD NO OVERT OFFICIAL LANGUAGE POLICY regulated by legal and constitutional declaration, yet it is the envy of many nations that aggressively police language use within their borders through explicit policies designed to protect the "purity" and "integrity" of the national language. They are envious that even without a rigid policy, the United States has managed to achieve such a high level of monolingualism and linguistic jingoism that speaking a language other than English constitutes a real liability. American monolingualism is part and parcel of an assimilationist ideology that decimated the American indigenous languages as well as the many languages brought to this shore by various waves of immigrants. As the mainstream culture felt threatened by the presence of multiple languages, which were perceived as competing with English, the reaction by the media, educational institutions, and government agencies was to launch periodic assaults on languages other than English. This was the case with American-Indian languages during the colonial period and German during the first and second world wars.

This covert assimilationist policy in the United States has been so successful in the creation of an ever-increasing linguistic xenophobia that most educators, including critical educators, have either blindly embraced the dominant assimilationist ideology or have remained ambivalent with respect to the worth of languages other than English. The assumption that English is a more viable and pedagogically suitable language than others has completely permeated U.S. educational discourse. Even though the advent of critical pedagogy has produced important debate concerning cultural democracy, social justice, and alternative ways of viewing the world, the question of language is, at best, rarely raised and, at worst, relegated to the margins. With the exception of a handful of critical educators who have taken seriously the role of language in enabling oppressed students to come to subjectivity, most critical educators have failed to engage in rigorous analyses that would unveil the intimate relationship between language, power, and ideology and the ensuing pedagogical consequences. Take, for example, the extensive literature in multicultural education, including critical multiculturalism. These writings usually assume that the valorization of ethnic cultures will take place only in English, of course. This assumption was bluntly interrogated by Donaldo Macedo and Lilia Bartolome when they argued that

> although the literature in multicultural education correctly stresses the need to valorize and appreciate cultural differences as a process for students to come to voice, the underlying assumption is that the celebration of other cultures will take place in English only, a language that may provide students from other linguistic and cultural backgrounds with the experience of subordination.[1]

Given this pervasive assimilationist culture it is not surprising that even well-intentioned critical educators fall prey to a seemingly laissez-faire language policy. As a result, most educators, including critical educators, not only see nothing wrong with their own monolingualism, they also give their tacit assent, sometimes unknowingly, to the reproduction of the English-only ideology. Conversely, they fail to understand that the ongoing debate about the effectiveness of bilingual education springs from an enormous misconception about the *nature* and *functions* of language. Opponents of bilingual education, conservative educators, and advocates of movements that support national and linguistic homogeneity and assimilation, assign to language a mechanistic, technical character. Within this technical perspective, they propose the adoption of English-only instruction as a remedy for the so-called "failure" of linguistic minority students. In addition, they claim that only through the mastery of English will non-English-speaking students be able to participate equally in mainstream society. However, the English-only remedy, or "English for the Children," as it has euphemistically redefined itself, seems to cure neither the symptom nor the cause of the problem. Reducing the bilingual education debate to technical issues of "teaching language" constitutes an assault on non-English-speaking students' cultural and ethnic identity, which is inextricably related to their language. It also veils the political and ideological nature of the issue. Viewing bilingual education as merely a technical language issue is, in reality, a complication rather than a simplification of the complex nature of the pedagogies required to address the specific linguistic and cultural needs of linguistic minority students. For language is not simply a technical system, a total of phonemes, morphemes, words and phrases, a code of signs of a particular form that enables members of a linguistic community to communicate. "Simple communication" implies linguistic interaction between humans in given historical, social, and cultural contexts. Humans are not machines or robots that simply produce grammatically correct phrases and exchange codified messages. Their way of communicating not only reflects, but also produces and/or reproduces, specific ideologies, as well as the feelings, values, and beliefs that invariably define their historical and social location. Identity is mapped onto language. In other words, individuals draw from a pool of social practices available to them in order to interpret (written/oral) "texts." Texts, in turn, as Norman Fairclough notes, "negotiate the sociocultural contradictions ... and more loosely 'differences' ... which are thrown up in social situations, and indeed they constitute a form in which social struggles are acted out."[2] Moreover, language is not merely reflective, and, as explained so eloquently by James Donald, educators must understand its productive nature.

> I take language to be productive rather than reflective of social reality. This means calling into question the assumptions that we, as speaking subjects, simply use language to organize and express our ideas and experiences. On the contrary, language is one of the most important social practices through which we come to experience ourselves as subjects. My point here is that once we get beyond the idea of language as no more than a medium of communication, as a tool equally available to all parties in cultural exchanges, then we can begin to examine language both as a practice of signification and also as a site for cultural struggle.[3]

As Donald points out, linguistic functions are not restricted to simple reflection or expression. Language actually shapes human existence in a dual way. For one, it affects the way humans are perceived through their speech. Secondly, individuals develop *discourses* that are formed through their identity in terms of class, race, gender, ethnicity, sexual orientation, popular culture, and other factors. Discourses should be understood, according to Fairclough, as "use[s] of language seen as a form of social practice,"[4] that is, as systems of communication shaped through historical, social, cultural, and ideological practices, which can work to either confirm or deny the life histories and experiences of the people who use them. Recognizing discourse as a social and ideological construct, James Gee defines it as "a socially accepted association among ways of using language, of thinking, and of acting that can be used to identify oneself as a member of a socially meaningful group or 'social network.'"[5] In what follows we want to argue that given the social and ideological nature of different functions and uses of language, the proposition that language is neutral or non-ideological constitutes, in reality, an ideological position itself.

Language as Ideology

The non-neutrality of language is very well understood by Jacques Derrida, who argues that even "everyday language is not innocent or neutral. ... It carries with it not only a considerable number of presuppositions of all types, but also presuppositions inseparable from metaphysics, which, although little attended to, are knotted into a system."[6] We would argue that the "metaphysics" to which Derrida refers can better be understood as ideological nets. Even if the functions of language are reduced to "mere communication," it still "presupposes subjects (whose identity and presence are constituted before the communication takes place) and objects (signified concepts, a thought meaning) that the passage of communication will have neither to constitute, nor, by all rights, to transform."[7]

As subjects of our language we possess a particular identity that is always crossed along the lines of race, ethnicity, class, gender, sexual orientation, and so forth. At the same time, as objects, we are marked by our language in terms of these same categories. In this sense, Pierre Bourdieu argues correctly that linguistic utterances or expressions are forms of practice and, as such, can be understood as the product of the relation between a linguistic *habitus* (a set of predispositions) and a linguistic market.[8] Linguistic utterances are produced in particular contexts or markets, and they always involve the speaker's socialized assessment of the market condition as well as the anticipations of this market. That is, all linguistic expression is a linguistic performance that addresses a particular market. For example, the U.S. linguistic market requires speakers to use so-called standard English, which is a valued and accepted linguistic variety for this particular market. A speaker of nonstandard English, e.g., Ebonics or "Spanglish," is not an acceptable speaker in the same market to the extent that he or she speaks a variety that is "inappropriate" and devalued by the dominant society. The highly charged debate in Oakland, California, over the recommendation to use Ebonics as a vehicle of instruction among African-American students in the public schools stands as formidable testimony to the power of linguistic hegemony in the U.S. market. Even middle-class African-Americans like Jesse Jackson became vocal adversaries of such pedagogical propositions, indicating the extent to which they have internalized the linguistic and cultural oppression perpetrated against them. Those African-Americans who oppose Ebonics as a viable vehicle of instruction in schools not only reflect a high level of colonization of the mind, but they also reinforce the yoke of the very colonialism that oppresses and represses their language—the most important signpost for cultural identity formation. Once African-Americans allow their minds to be colonized, they are unable to "examine language both as a practice of signification and as a site for cultural struggle—a mechanism which produces antagonistic relations between different social groups."[9]

Linguistic oppression is not necessarily restricted to speakers of nonstandard varieties. An alleged speaker of standard English who, for example, has not received formal education may turn out to be a nonacceptable speaker at certain levels of linguistic interaction (e.g., at a corporate board meeting or in academia). Bourdieu illustrates this point by saying that individuals from upper-class backgrounds are endowed with a linguistic habitus—tied to a specific kind of cultural capital—that enables them to respond with relative ease to the demands of most formal or official occasions. This includes obviously the school curriculum. On the other hand, he adds, "Individuals from petit-bourgeois backgrounds must generally make an effort to adapt their linguistic expressions to the demands of formal markets. The result is that their speech is often accompanied by tension and anxiety, and by a tendency to rectify or correct expressions so that they concur with dominant norms."[10]

The notion of "habitus" can also be understood as a form of "apprenticeship, that is, socially learned discourse and behavior that can either deny or affirm access to particular social and cultural practices. Individuals who have been apprenticed through particular discourses to approach the dominant "norm" become competent speakers of the standard, while members who develop discourses that diverge from the "norm" are perceived as speaking nonstandard varieties. In either case, whenever language is present, an invisible but omnipresent evaluation system is put into play. Therefore, the set of predispositions—namely the cultural capital (as different forms of cultural knowledge, including language knowledge) that shapes one's discourse—differs among individuals. Through linguistic interaction, evaluation functions not only to measure an individual's "value"—in terms of what the language actually "says" about the speaker—but also classifies individuals into preconceived groups identified as speaking nonacceptable languages for the respective markets. As a result, language evaluation is an inherent mechanism that is often used to dominate other groups culturally. This mechanism was used effectively by the colonial powers, and its legacy remains anchored in the current language policies of former colonial possessions, particularly in Africa, where the official languages with more currency are always the colonial languages. In some real sense, the language policy in the United States functions as a form of internal colonialism. Hence, even if non-English-speaking students are able to meet the needs of the U.S. linguistic market (in terms of mastering enough English to "simply communicate," as the proponents of English-only suggest), they will still be identified as the "other." Their language will always be marked by their color, race, ethnicity, and class and constructed within a politics of identity that situates subjects within an assimilation grid. Generally, groups of speakers who are typecast via the devaluation of their language tend to resort to resistance by protecting their only tools of opposing domination, namely language and culture. In short, their language will always be marked by their otherness, both in terms of ways they are perceived and the ways they see the world ideologically. Thus, it becomes obvious that the issue at hand is not language, but the right to be different in a supposed cultural democracy. Or as Fairclough accurately notes, "the problematic of language and power is fundamentally a question of democracy."[11] However, the issue here is not simply to acknowledge cultural diversity. As Homi Bhabha reminds us, cultural difference—as opposed to cultural diversity[12]—should be understood as

> the awareness that first of all you have the problem of difference, not because there are many preconstituted cultures. ... Cultural difference is a particular constructed discourse at a time when something is being challenged about power or authority. At that point, a particular cultural trait or tradition ... becomes the site of contestation, abuse, insult, and discrimination. Cultural difference is not the natural emanation of the fact that there are different cultures in the world. It's a much more problematic and sophisticated reproduction of a ritual, a habit, a trait, a characteristic ...

> The question of cultural difference is not the problem of there being diverse cultures and that diversity produces the

difference. It is that each time you want to make a judgment about a culture or about a certain element within a certain culture in the context of some kind of social and political condition that puts pressure on that judgment, you are standing at that point in this disjunctive difference-making site.

Through the proposition that the English language is a passport which gives access to the higher cultural, political, and economic echelons of U.S. society, opponents of bilingual education attempt to hide their ongoing cultural invasion of other groups. Learning standard English will not iron out social stratification, racism, and xenophobia. Nevertheless, under the "naivete" pretext and the notion that language exists in a vacuum, conservative educators continue to disarticulate language from its social and ideological context by conveniently ignoring the following facts:

First, *meaning carried by language can never be analyzed in an isolated fashion.* Meaning is always historically constructed, and it is a phenomenon of culture, a product of culture that is inherently ideological and, thus, political. Furthermore, as everything ideological possesses meaning, every sign—as a form of meaning—is also ideological. Following this line of argument, access to meaning must invariably involve a process whereby the reading of the world must precede the reading of the word. That is to say, to access the meaning of an entity, we must understand the cultural practices that mediate our access to the world semantic field and its interaction with the words' semantic features.

Second, *language cannot exist apart from its speakers.* The transition from the Sassurean "langue" to "parole " is possible only through the mediation of humans as agents of history who actively participate in the formation and transformation of their world. Human communication is unique; human language is "species-specific" and cannot simply exist in a form of abstract signs. It is humans that give meaning to the signs, where the signifier becomes the signified. Language cannot exist as an autonomous code, detached from its speakers and contexts. By neglecting the role of the speaker in his/her cultural, political, and ideological location and by ignoring the context in which communication takes place (the parameters set in the linguistic market), we fail to acknowledge that language, in all of its aspects, can by no means be either neutral or innocent. It is a social as well as a cultural marker.

Roland Barthes makes the claim that "to decipher the world's signs always means to struggle with a certain innocence of objects."[13] This ostensible innocence of objects must be challenged in order to conceptualize language in its real dimension and to position the debate on bilingual education within its ideological and political context. The real context of the debate has nothing to do with language itself, but with what language carries in terms of cultural goods. As Bhabha reminds us,"there is some particular issue about the redistribution of goods between cultures, or the funding of cultures, or the emergence of minorities or immigrants in a situation of resources—where resource allocation has to go— or the construction of schools and the decision about whether the school should be bilingual or trilingual or whatever. It is at that point that the problem of cultural difference is produced."[14]

If Bhabha is correct, then linguists and educators need to move beyond the notion that language is a "treasure," a common possession—what Bourdieu calls "the illusion of linguistic communism."[15] The existence of a common language, a "code" open to use by everybody and equally accessible to all—as assumed by proponents of the English-only movement—is illusionary. This assumption begs the question of why, from a sea of languages, "dialects," "standards," and "varieties," standard English emerged as the most appropriate and viable tool of institutional communication. Application of the simple theorem that "language is identified with its speakers" would require that we find native speakers of standard English, identify them, and analyze their "mother tongue." I am convinced that no American is a native speaker of "Harvard English," and definitely no French person has the discourse of the Académie Française as his or her mother tongue. If mastery of standard English is a prerequisite for enjoying the "common culture," we first need to clarify what kind of standard English we are to teach and thus to speak. This statement seems to contradict itself, as some would argue that there are not many kinds of standard English. Standard English would literally be "clear" English, sterilized from any "familiarity," "jargons," or "unacceptable" forms that "dialects" often use, the kind of English used in the "Great Books." In addition, the existence and use of a "colorless and odorless," sterilized code implies that language is dehistoricized and that we, as humans, have no obvious markers of identity (such as ethnicity, culture, race, class, gender, or sexual orientation) reflected and refracted through our language. A more honest definition would address the following questions: "Who speaks the standard?" "Who has access to it?" "Where does one develop this particular discourse and through what process of apprenticeship?"

Those who assume a "common culture" invariably imply the existence of a common language. This is evident when Ronald Wardaugh asserts that "language is a *communal possession,* although admittedly an abstract one. Individuals have access to it and constantly show that they do so by using it properly. ... A wide range of skills and activities is subsumed under this concept of *proper use.*"[16] However, Wardaugh's position raises a series of problems. If language is a common treasure among humans, how can we explain the fact that some languages are perceived as more "appropriate" or even more "civilized" than others? Why are there "standard" languages? Why are some languages considered "well-chosen," "sophisticated," "elevated," or "civilized," while others are "familiar," "uncouth," "popular," "patois," "varieties," "crude," or "pidgin"? If language is a communal possession, why is it that, although every human being possesses a language, not every language is perceived as "human"? For example, pidgin and creole languages are usually characterized as savage, corrupt, or bastardized forms of colonial languages. How is it that the use of human language can work towards dehumanizing certain cultural groups? If everybody has a language, how is it that some people, although they have a language, don't have a voice, and as a result, need to be interpreted in order to emerge from their silenced culture? And if language is nothing but a communication tool, how can we explain the phenomenon of linguistic imposition of one language in preference to another, as well as the fact that some languages are held up as models to which others ought to aspire? If language is so innocent, why in most countries is linguistic policy part of governments' self-interest? Why do people work and fight for language conservation and propagation throughout the world? If language is a shared good, how is legitimacy granted to the process of robbing some people of their own language? Moreover, who defines the "proper" use to which Wardaugh was referring? If speakers of a language have equal access to this illusionary common code, why do we not all speak the same variety—namely the standard?

These questions can be answered only if language is assigned to its real ideological and social context, and the mechanisms of linguistic and cultural oppression are unveiled. As Paulo Freire suggested, "For cultural invasion to succeed, it is essential that those invaded become convinced of their intrinsic inferiority ... The more invasion is accentuated and those invaded are alienated from the spirit of their own culture and from themselves, the more the latter want to be like the invaders: to walk like them, talk like them."[17]

Since language is always intertwined with culture, cultural invasion is intimately tied to linguistic invasion. Language is culture. The language policy of the United States—which gave rise to the English-only movement and the more recent "English for the Children" idea, as well as the incessant debate over bilingual education—clearly illustrates the mechanism of linguistic and cultural hegemony in process. The dominant ideology requires a homogenized standard language and labels other forms as "dialects," "jargons," or "patois." This process legitimizes the standard as the norm, and that, in turn, benefits a dominant order. When the standard becomes the norm, it serves as the yardstick against which all other linguistic varieties are measured. This evaluation process will invariably lead to forms of devaluation, which are almost always connected to factors of culture, ethnicity, class, gender, and race. Through this process, the dominant ideology works to devalue any form of "different" or "popular" language, or language of a "different color." The same ideology labels African-American English as nonstandard and creates the perception that it is an incomprehensible dialect, occurring only in black ghettos, and that one can easily produce it by simply breaking the rules of standard English.[18] As mentioned earlier, the incredible intolerance for different varieties of language was clearly demonstrated a few years ago in the debate over Ebonics or black English. The mainstream mass media and public opinion totally rejected this form of linguistic and cultural "otherness" and manifested their inherent racism in their constant devaluation of Ebonics. In this context it is not an exaggeration to speak about linguistic hegemony to the extent that the development of a normative discourse through standard English naturalizes, for instance, ideologies and practices connected to white supremacy, racism, and oppression. According to Fairclough, "naturalized discourse conventions are a most effective mechanism for sustaining and reproducing cultural and ideological dimensions of hegemony."[19]

Moreover, as language is identified with its speakers, it is obvious why oppressed and marginalized ethnic or cultural groups are perceived as speaking a nonstandard or "second-class" language, a "dialect" that does not deserve to be heard or taught and which is always associated with backwardness or savageness. It is also obvious why the speakers of those languages are perceived as not being "endowed" with the "linguistic habitus" required to address the needs of the U.S. linguistic market. The real target in the English-only debate is not the language spoken by these cultural groups but their humanity and cultural identity. The debate should be unmasked to reveal its inhumanity, unfairness, dishonesty, and outrageousness.

Identification of language with human culture sheds light on every attempt to impose English on students from diverse linguistic and cultural backgrounds. This particular practice is not new; it has been implemented and tested for centuries through colonization. Integration into a single "linguistic community" is a product of political domination. Institutions capable of imposing universal recognition of a dominant language recognize this process as a means for establishing relations of linguistic domination and colonization.

As we have suggested, the existence of a common language also implies the existence of a common culture. Conversely, any reference to a common culture must also imply the existence of an uncommon culture. Donaldo Macedo analyzed this dialectical relationship in *Literacies of Power*:

> The conservative cultural agenda fails to acknowledge ... that the reorganization of 'our common culture' points to the existence of 'our uncommon culture,' for commonality is always in a dialectical relationship with uncommonality. Thus, one cannot talk about the centeredness of our 'common culture' without relegating our 'uncommon' cultural values and expressions to the margins, creating a de facto silent majority.[20]

What supporters of the English-only movement and opponents of bilingual education wish to achieve through the imposition of a "common culture" is the creation of a de facto silent majority. Since language is so intertwined with culture, any call for a "common culture" must invariably require the existence of a "common language." In fact, the English-only proponents' imposition of standard English as the only viable vehicle of communication in our society's institutional and civic life, under the rubric of our "common language," inevitably leads to the "tongue-tying of America." This "tongue-tying" aids the conservative attempt to reproduce dominant cultural values by insisting, on one hand, on ever-present, collective myths that present a diverse origin, a diverse past, and diverse ancestors, and, on the other, on a common mother tongue and a necessary common, homogeneous, and indivisible future.[21] In general, movements that claim to promote ethnic, linguistic, and cultural integrity attempt, in reality, to impose cultural domination through linguistic domination, under the guise of an assimilative and let's-live-all-together-happily model. This process invariably becomes a form of stealing one's language, which is like stealing one's history, one's culture, one's own life. As Ngugi Wa' Thiongo so clearly points out:

> Communication between human beings is the basis and process of evolving culture. Values are the basis of people's identity, their sense of particularity as members of the human race. All this is carried by language. Language as culture is the collective memory bank of a people's experience in history. Culture is almost indistinguishable from the language that makes possible its genesis, growth, banking, articulation, and indeed its transmission from one generation to the next.[22]

If Ngugi is correct, and we believe he is, all of society is permeated by language. Therefore, in a certain sense, everything is cultural; it is impossible to be part of a non-culture, as it is impossible to be part of a non-language. When a dominant group cuts out the possibility of language transmission from one generation to the next by imposing its own language under the guise of a "common language," it also cuts out the cultural sequence and, therefore, cuts people from their cultural roots. So far we have attempted to argue that, in reality, there is no such thing as a "common culture" in multicultural American society. In fact, it is an oxymoron to speak of a "common culture" in a cultural democracy. In truth, there was never a "common culture" in which people of all races and colors participated equally in the United States. Hence, the proposition "common culture" is a euphemism that has been used to describe the imposition of Western dominant culture in order to eliminate, degrade, and devalue any different ethnic/cultural/class characteristics. It is a process through which the dominant social groups attempt to achieve cultural hegemony by imposing a mythical "common language." In turn, language is often used by the dominant groups as a manipulative tool to achieve hegemonic control. As a result, the current debate over bilingual education has very little to do with language per se. The real issue that undergirds the English-only movements is the economic, social, and political control by a dominant minority of a largely subordinate majority which no longer fits the profile of what it means to be part of "our common culture" and to speak "our common language."

The English-only movements' call for a "common language" does more than hide a pernicious social and cultural agenda. It is also part of an attempt to reorganize a "cultural hegemony," as evidenced by the unrelenting attack of conservative educators on multicultural education and curriculum diversity. The assault by conservatives on the multiplicity of languages spoken in the United States is part of the dominant cultural agenda to both promote a monolithic ideology and to eradicate any and all forms of cultural expression that do not conform to the promoted monolithic ideology. This reproductive mechanism is succinctly explained by Henry Giroux, when he shows how the conservative cultural revolution's

> more specific expressions have been manifest on a number of cultural fronts including schools, the art world, and the more blatant attacks aimed at rolling back the benefits of civil rights and social welfare reforms constructed over the last three decades. What is being valorized in the dominant language of the culture industry is an undemocratic approach to social authority and a politically regressive move to reconstruct American life within the script of Eurocentrism, racism, and patriarchy.[23]

What becomes clear in our discussion so far is that the current bilingual education debate has very little to do with teaching or not teaching English to non-English speakers. The real issue has a great deal more to do with the hegemonic forces that aggressively want to maintain the present asymmetry in the distribution of cultural and economic goods.

Schools and the Reproduction of Legitimate Language

An understanding of the nature and functions of language is crucial in order to locate areas of public life and institutions that actually reproduce the so-called legitimate language. Habermas correctly urges us "not to limit our critique on relationships of power to those institutions in which power is overtly declared, hence to political and social power only; we must extend it to those areas of life in which power is hidden behind the *amiable countenance of cultural familiarity.*"[24] It is necessary to identify mechanisms of domination in order to make their ideology bare.

Educational institutions show this "amiable countenance of cultural familiarity," while at the same time, playing a crucial role in the perpetuation of linguistic domination—the cultural reproduction inherent in any form of standardization process. Despite the widespread conservative notion that schools are, or at least should be, temples of neutrality and objectivity, the claim of neutrality hides a conservative view which perceives knowledge as neutral and pedagogy as "a transparent vehicle of truth." This perception "overlooks important political issues regarding how canons are historically produced, whose interests they serve as well as whose they do not serve, and how they are sustained within specific forms of institutional power."[25]

Schools as sites of struggle and contestation that reproduce the dominant culture and ideology, as well as what is perceived as legitimate language/knowledge, make use of their institutional power to either affirm or deny a learner's language, and thus his or her lived experiences and culture. Additionally, schools are not simply static institutions that mirror the social order or reproduce the dominant ideology. They are active agents in the very construction of the social order and the dominant ideology. In that sense linguistic jingoism is constructed and spread within educational institutions through curricula, textbooks, etc. Educational institutions, in their symbolic and material existence, are so powerful that Althusser considers them to be "the dominant ideological State apparatus[es]."[26] He further explains that "no other apparatus has the obligatory audience of the totality of the children in the capitalistic social formation, eight hours a day, for five or six days out of seven."[27] While Althusser's position collapses into a theory of domination that does not allow for any type of resistance or radical forms of pedagogy, he is correct when he insists that the meaning of schools should be understood within the context of ideological state apparatuses.

Schools, throughout history, have directly helped to devalue popular modes of expression, as well as "varieties" or "dialects." They have also served to elevate the standard language as the most clear and appropriate variety. This process has been implemented partly through the invisibility, falsification, or marginalization of "otherness," which is usually subsumed under the "common" rubric. Schools as sites where legitimate knowledge and language are reproduced have promoted a "deficit view" of learners from different linguistic and cultural backgrounds, managing thus to impose a linguistic norm that defines a socially recognized criterion of linguistic "correctness." As sites of cultural reproduction, schools have constantly denied the experiences of specific groups of students from diverse linguistic and cultural backgrounds, making sure to transmit what counts as knowledge, namely Western culture, so as to ensure national assimilation and preserve Western dominance in the curriculum. Through particular educational practices, the doctrinal system in the United States manages to promote the instruction of English as a necessary prerequisite in order to participate "equally" in the mainstream society. In reality, this requirement functions invariably as a barrier that prevents non-English speakers from having equal access to education and knowledge. This barrier prevents non-English speakers and other subordinate cultural groups from having access to the higher economic and social echelons of our society. It is important to point out that knowledge is not exclusive to English and that bodies of knowledge can be both produced and learned in other languages. To do otherwise is to consider English as education in itself. The facile English-only solution is illusionary to the extent that, in the mainstream, non-whites and students who belong to subordinate classes are deprived of access to quality education. Educational policy in the United States reflects an implicit economic need to socialize immigrants and members of oppressed groups to fill necessary but undesirable, low-status jobs.[28] In reality, instead of the democratic education the United States claims to provide, what is in place is a sophisticated colonial model of education designed primarily to train state functionaries and commissars who work for private ideological interests while denying access to millions. The result is to further exacerbate the equity gap already victimizing a great number of so-called minority students. The majority of whites who do not speak standard English because of their class position are also victims of this model of U.S. democracy. They are strategically taught that they belong to the norm, though they themselves are exploited, excluded, and devalued.

In addition to the function of cultural reproduction, educators should pay closer attention to the cultural production that takes place within schools—a process that affirms the individual's daily, lived experiences and which could tend toward "collective self-determination." As Giroux so eloquently argues, "[i]t is essential ... to move from questions of social and cultural reproduction to issues of social and cultural production, from the question of how society gets reproduced in the interest of the capital and its institutions to the question of how the 'excluded majorities' have and can develop institutions, values, and practices that serve their autonomous interests."[29]

It is only through cultural production (and this includes one's own language behaviors) that one can come to subjectivity. This is a process through which linguistic minority students, by speaking their own language, gain authorship of their world and are enabled to move from their present object to a subject position. However, this movement cannot occur unless progressive educators acquire critical tools that would facilitate the development of a thorough understanding of the mechanisms employed by the dominant culture in the reproduction of those ideological elements that devalue, disconfirm, and subjugate cultural and linguistic minority students. It is only "through an understanding of hegemony and cultural invasion, [that] critical bicultural educators can create culturally democratic environments where they can assist students to identify the different ways that domination and oppression have an impact on their lives."[30] Bilingual/multicultural education has to be situated within a theory of cultural production and viewed as an integral part of the way in which people produce, transform, and reproduce meaning.

Bilingual and multicultural education must also be seen as a medium that constitutes and affirms the historical and existential moments of lived experience which produce a subordinate or a lived culture.

Within this framework of action, language cannot be seen only as a neutral tool for communication. It should be viewed as the only means through which learners make sense of their world and transform it in the process of meaning-making. In the meaning-making process, both subordinate students and their teachers need to know that standard English is "the oppressor's language yet I need it to talk to you."[31] As bell hooks so painfully understands, standard English "is the language of conquest and domination ... it is the mask which hides the loss of so many tongues, all those sounds of diverse, native communities we will never hear."[32]

All those teachers who consider themselves agents of change and who struggle to create a more democratic culture need a thorough understanding of the role of standard English—even when minority students must acquire it in order to capture its dominance and re-create it as a counter-hegemonic force. Their struggle needs to highlight how standard English is used "as a weapon to silence and censor."[33] In order to avoid the tongue-tying, silencing, and censorship that the use of standard English creates, we need to heed the analysis of language and its role in sabotaging democracy as recounted by June Jordan:

> I am talking about majority problems of language in a democratic state, problems of a currency that someone has stolen and hidden away and then homogenized into an official "English" language that can only express non-events involving nobody responsible, or lies. If we lived in a democratic state our language would have to hurtle, fly, curse, and sing, in all the common American names, all the undeniable and representative participating voices of everybody here. We would

not tolerate the language of the powerful and, thereby, lose all respect for words, per se. We would make our language conform to the truth of our many selves and we would make our language lead us into the equality of power that a democratic state must represent.[34]

II

EUROPEAN DISCOURSES OF HOMOGENIZATION IN THE DISCOURSE OF LANGUAGE PLANNING[1]

⟳

DURING THE LAST TEN YEARS OR SO, A CENTRAL THEME IN RESEARCH concerning language planning has been motivated by a contradiction for which there is no single or simple resolution. It concerns the European Union as a supranational state that, on the one hand, articulates its commitment to respecting the linguistic and cultural diversity of its members, and on the other, propagates linguistic and cultural uniformity. The English language as ruler and the other "strong" languages sustain domination over the "weak" ones. Interestingly, linguistic hegemony in Europe has been assisted in the past by language education planning and is aided at present by curricular practices in European schools of both the Center and the Periphery.

Given that linguistic hegemony originates and results in the unequal distribution of wealth and of cultural and political power, this situation is potentially alarming. It poses a threat to the unity of Europe, the plurilingual future of which seems bleak. Without doubt, English is on its way to becoming the sole language for international relations, intellectual production, mass communication, technology, and so on.[2] Indeed, it is likely that the "mighty force of English" will become so great that it will unofficially become Europe's *lingua franca*. This monolingualism is predominantly viewed as an easy solution to what is construed as a communication problem. However, there are a few of us who are convinced that it would be a serious error to underestimate the long-term social effects that such a solution is bound to bring, in particular, the impact of such encroachment on the linguistic and cultural rights of member states in the Periphery.

Posing the Problem

Recognizing the complexity and multiplicity of reasons why linguistic hegemony prevails in Europe, and not underestimating the structural conditions that make it seem inevitable, we want here to concentrate on the discursive practices which facilitate it. This chapter will focus on European language-planning discourse, critical analysis of which reveals that its *raison d'être* has been to resolve social conflict assumed to originate in linguistic and cultural heterogeneity. The result is neutralization, a legitimization of particular valuations concerning languages and language varieties that lead to monolingual cultural choices. The important point is that in order to understand the logic on which the discourse of language planning is based, one needs to deconstruct and genealogize other discourses which are inscribed therein. It is indeed true that language planning involves a composite of sociopolitical discourses that have developed within the Western tradition of humanism and rationality—a tradition obsessed with identity, singleness, and purity. It is this tradition which has given birth to the academic discourses that inform the disciplines of linguistics, language education, and curriculum theory.

What follows is a brief review of the basic discursive practices of these disciplines from a critical perspective. We wish to show that each of them separately, and all of them together, have been based on what Jacques Derrida calls an "ethics of sameness," rather than an "ethics of difference."[3] Furthermore, we will argue that they are all based on a "philosophy of the same" which entails "fear of the Other." They do not utilize a "discourse of difference," which emphasizes heterogeneity in order ultimately to protect the Other.[4] Our basic claim is that, infiltrated by these discourses, the discursive practices of language planning in Europe construe linguistic and cultural homogeneity in positive terms and diversity negatively, thus impeding plurilingual perspectives in Europe.

Defining the Concept of Discourse

In mainstream linguistics the term *discourse* has been defined as "written or spoken language, which has been produced in the act of communication."[5] We do not adhere to this view and feel obliged to make this clear here. Our understanding of discourse draws upon the notion formulated by Michel Foucault, who does not view it in linguistic terms. In his early work, Foucault proposes an "archaeology of knowledge" by analyzing *orders of discourse,* which for him are the different disciplines (i.e., the *epistemes*) that shape conditions of knowledge. Each *order* (that is, each discourse) is bound by regulations, which are enforced through social practices, and it exhibits immanent principles of regularity.[6] In this sense, discourse is a regulated formation of expression, of discursive practices. Each discourse forms an "archive," a law of regularity, a system of knowledge, linked to the operation of the nondiscursive practice of social power.[7] The conditions of possibility of these practices are at the same time their conditions for existence.[8] Hence, through discourse analysis one hopes to reconstruct the conditions for discursive practices as formations of knowledge systems. This is attempted presently, as we examine other discourses within the discourse of language planning.

Language Planning as a Discipline

Language planning emerged as an academic discipline in its own right in the 1950s. It influenced social and cultural factors by dressing contemporaneous assumptions in the robe of scientific neutrality and correctness, suppressing ideological contradictions. As an integral feature of government-authorized language policy, with which the state aims to achieve conformity and thus legitimate its power, language planning focuses on the distribution of linguistic power and involves planners as wielders of sociocultural and economic power in a state, a nation, or a nationalizing entity. In fact, the unquestioned right of a state to interfere with language rights and to determine the official language is bound intimately to the notion of the state. As Pierre Bourdieu argues, it is the process of state formation that creates conditions for the constitution of a unified linguistic market, dominated by an official language.[9] This dominant language, used on official occasions and in official places, becomes the norm against which all linguistic practices are theoretically measured.

Linguistic domination is intrinsically connected with the power of language to create meaning and legitimate communicative norms. The power of language to construct subjectivity and social reality makes it a site of both ideological and political struggle. The language planning discipline has been at the heart of such struggle. Presenting itself as a science and claiming scientific objectivity, its discourse has facilitated the development of commonsense notions related to linguistic domination, the legitimization of assimilationist values, and the authority of the state. It has construed the nation as a speech community, undifferentiated and united, with a national language existing to serve its entire population. It claims that lack of such a common language inhibits communication and thus generates conflict— thereby implying that conflict is a result not of economic but of linguistic differentiation. This is clearly the argument used in the neoliberal discourse of economic forces in Europe. The blaming of economic fragmentation on linguistic differences is also evident in the English-only debate in the United States and in the controversy over the official language in Canada.

This claim is commonplace in language planning discourse, which has, by and large, uncritically adopted the argument that economic development is best achieved in linguistic and culturally homogeneous states. This argument is sustained on the basis of assumptions developed particularly when Europe was in search of social order after the crisis of the industrial revolution. According to these assumptions, order is best represented through homogeneity, while conflict derives from difference.[10] As a theoretical hypothesis, this claim has been supported in numerous academic texts by sociolinguists considered authorities in the field of language planning. Joshua Fishman, for example, has argued that linguistic homogeneity is a basic characteristic of states that are economically more developed, educationally more advanced, politically more modernized, and ideologically/politically more tranquil and stable.[11] Similar arguments by other theorists frequently fail to take into account important structural factors which constitute the conditions for economic development and political stability in particular countries. They also consistently disregard the cases of plurilingual communities in which the imposition of monolingualism has undermined educational and economic development and ultimately threatened political tranquillity, as in most African countries that adopted the colonizers' language as their official language. As a result, most Africans can only access education through foreign languages, languages that may provide many Africans with the experience of subordination. Williams[12] points out that a number of sociolinguistic studies indicate that a shared language may be accompanied by social division rather than integration. Yet despite these findings, language planning discourse has continued to project as somehow irrational any resistance to the process of language unification.[13] Such thinking creates fertile ground in the European Union today for discursive practices that present the idea of a plurilingual suprastate as both unrealistic and economically unproductive.

The association between language and nation has a long history.[14] So have the values handed down to us through popular slogans such as *one language-one nation*. The belief that a single and unified variety of language symbolizes the unity of a nation is quite strong, particularly in communities whose cultural and linguistic practices are threatened by unstable sociopolitical circumstances. This belief and the general conflation of race, culture, and language are rooted in the eighteenth- and nineteenth-century search for the cultural origins of human populations. Consequently cultivated by European thought, which has construed language as the "mirror of the nation," this discourse could perhaps be linked to the Enlightenment belief in a shared reason and harmony constituting a common human essence. It is part of the Western tradition of humanism and rationality, a tradition obsessed with identity, singleness, and purity, operating to shape homogenizing ideologies. Discursive practices have construed beliefs that only unified, homogeneous entities—be they selves or states—can act effectively. But, as McGowan asserts in reference to Kant's philosophical project, "[t]he effect of designating universal conditions of rationality that define the essentially human is to exclude various differences as, by definition, nonhuman."[15] Derrida has called this persistence of homogenizing thought "Western metaphysics" or the "philosophy of the same," as it entails "fear of the Other." This fear, he says, is always constitutive of totalizing systems.[16]

Discourses of Linguistics

The ideology of homogenization has been sustained by other academic discourses that inform the discipline of language planning. Against a background where all people were viewed as a homogeneous group with common characteristics, traits, ideals, and norms, disciplinary discourses represented language as a collective cultural memory of its speakers. For example, the main paradigm in so-called theoretical linguistics—the discipline which emerged in the twentieth century claiming scientific objectivity for itself—language came to be viewed as autonomized, self-defining, and self-contained, delimiting nations and national character. Furthermore, linguistics defined language as a fixed system, amenable to analysis—a definition that excluded the social, cultural, and political implications of language use.

We are referring to two influential trends in linguistics. One developed on the basis of Ferdinand de Saussure's conception of *la langue* and his idealization of the community of the nation-state. The other stems from the generativists' concept of a homogeneous speech community and of the "ideal speaker-hearer." As Harris rightly observes, Saussure "evidently saw the linguistically 'normal' individual as being monoglot, and the linguistically 'normal' community as being a monoglot community. Bilingualism and plurilingualism are apparently 'unnatural' conditions for Saussure, and he never discusses them."[17] Noam Chomsky, on the other hand, who presents language as a unitary innate system, relegates all variation to the random vagaries of performance. Such influential views facilitated the formulation of the norm of monolingualism, which, as Alastair Pennycook argues, became "a legacy of very particular political and cultural circumstances in Europe."[18] In fact, Pennycook provides an enlightening account of linguistics and applied linguistics as a very particular European cultural form, adhering to principles of positivism and structuralism.[19] We agree with his conclusion that the cultural politics of linguistics has produced a view of language as an isolated structural entity.

Sociolinguistics as a whole, and particularly what is often referred to as the "ethnography of speaking," has equal responsibility for sustaining concepts regarding ethnolinguistic homogeneity. For example, Dell Hymes and M. Saville-Troike advocate a comparative approach to cross-cultural communication studies which is based on notions of language as an ethnically homogeneous unity, ultimately implying perhaps that language is ethnogenic.[20] Comparative and contrastive studies of speech, such as those by Blum-Kulka and Olshtain, Maria Sifianou, and Deborah Tannen, among many others, view culture as a collectivist phenomenon which explains the totality of belief and behavior of the individual as a member of the ethnic group.[21] They focus on explaining differences in the linguistic behavior of speech communities, as though each were a homogeneous group. They disregard social differentiation on the basis of class, age, gender, etc., and exclude from their analysis the institutional use of language. Ultimately, they also fail to address the distinction between ethnicity and ethnic group. Language in these studies is the embodiment of ethnicity and associated with the concept of an ethnolinguistic group.

These discourses from the domain of linguistics have definitely infiltrated the discourse of language planning, which has represented linguistic and cultural heterogeneity as unnatural. The discipline's motivating purpose is to create social order by establishing some form of homogeneity. Indeed, the *raison d'être* of language planning is to resolve social conflict and bring social order by legitimating particular valuations concerning languages and language varieties. Though its discursive practices are assumed to be shaped by different ideologies resulting in choices between linguistic assimilationism, vernacularization, internationalization, and linguistic pluralism,[22] critical analysis shows that ultimately all discursive choices in language planning aim at some form of homogenization rather than at the legitimization of differentiation and the recognition of cultural and linguistic pluralism as socially valuable.

Linguistic homogeneity is most frequently achieved with language education planning and educational policies, which reinforce relations of power and often formalize political developments. Even in societies that officially recognize linguistic pluralism, educational language planning ultimately aims at a particular form of assimilationism, since no other language is ascribed equal status with the official or national language, and "minority" languages and their users are frequently seen as inferior or subordinate.

Discourses of Curriculum and Language Education Planning

Issues of language in school curricula, planning, and policymaking are intertwined with ideological meanings within the context of the cultural politics of language. Whether the official/national language is offered as a first language, a second or a foreign language, and how and which other languages are included or excluded from the school curriculum are questions tightly connected to broader sociopolitical issues. Yet, as Susan Sontag and T. S. Donahue both argue, many analyses of language planning and language policy in education have failed to make a critical examination of the political strategies adopted by those involved in these social practices.[23]

Only recently has concern emerged about the strong relationship between language policy and language education, with particular emphasis on power and inequality. It is based on the understanding that language is the basic resource through which learners gain access to knowledge; fashion experience, values, and attitudes; organize and build their world; develop an understanding of social reality; and come to regard some things as valuable and others as worthless. This view raises the question of how a language, which is naturally stratified and diverse, is represented in the school curriculum. Or is it? The relevant literature indicates that it is not represented. Actually, it seems that one primary aim in educational language planning is to silence the living heteroglossia and impose a standard language—one single discourse ratified by schools and other official institutions. Putting this aim into effect results in limiting the polyphonic nature of language and fixing a homogeneous order of perception and expression—a process which can be described in Bakhtinian terms as "ideological closure."

The very purpose of national curriculum planning in the West has been to reinstate and reaffirm nationally shared knowledges and values, and its goal has been to produce subjects with a national identity. Hence, the discourse of educational planning has consistently projected the social role of the curriculum as that of developing a high degree of normative and cognitive consensus among the elements of society. In this way, diverse social groups can finally be embraced as part of the narrative of the national culture, without disturbing its norms. In other words, educational planning aspires to erase difference. Difference is represented as unproductive, as a threat to stability, tradition and culture, and is viewed as a finite and self-sufficient body of values, customs, and traditions. The structural inequalities of power in practice are generally not acknowledged, while social, ethnic, and linguistic differences are construed as potentially subversive. Therefore, the dominant discourse of curriculum planning has not concerned itself with the challenges and opportunities posed by an exploration of difference—not individual difference, nor difference based on hierarchical ordering and binary oppositions, but difference as social multiplicity, heterogeneity, and contradiction. Most publications in the field suggest ways of overcoming or erasing difference. There are far too few of them proposing that school curricula be restructured so that they may address the needs of the groups traditionally excluded from the dominant discourse of schooling. And few suggest that literacy be redefined as a form of cultural politics based on difference. Proposals advocated by critical educators such as Henry Giroux and Paulo Freire would serve the purpose of incorporating cultural, linguistic, and social differences into the

ongoing pedagogical project.[24] However, such concerns are strikingly absent from curriculum planning, while concerns with
knowledge seen as objective and value-free are very present. In
fact, the mainstream discourse of curriculum planning has construed knowledge as neutral, although it is effectively composed
of the meanings and values of the dominant culture which are
naturalized in such a way that people acquiring this knowledge
see no other alternatives to the social, cultural, and economic
reality.

As becomes evident from the above, the question of knowledge—which, as John Fiske argues, does not exist in an empir-
icist, objective relationship to the real and is thus never neutral—is
depoliticized in the discourse of the discipline.[25] Largely informed
by theories of the psychology of learning, which are characterized by their apolitical and ahistorical perspectives, the main
goals of the discipline are related to teaching methodologies,
learning strategies, and pupils' achievements. Such concerns result in the reduction of political and ideological questions about
knowledge to a mere "how to." Questions about *what* or *whose*
knowledge is to be transmitted in schools, *who selects* this knowledge and *why,* what the *reasons* are that it is organized the way
it is, and *why* are seldom raised.[26]

Such important questions seem particularly relevant in foreign language curricula and syllabus planning. In posing them,
language education planners are denaturalizing choices, which
more often than not are a result of hegemonic processes. An-
swering these questions, i.e., in making decisions about what
foreign languages are to be taught in schools and how, entails
involvement with the politics of foreign language education—a
field that has by and large developed in apolitical terms. However, it is important for curriculum planners to politicize questions
of foreign language education—to ask, for instance, *what language knowledge* counts as legitimate, *whose language* is important enough to be included in the curriculum, *why,* and *in what*

terms. For example, in Greece, which has a growing economic-immigrant population, it would seem important to problematize the reasons why the Greek language is not offered by the state school system as a second or as a foreign language. And supposing it were, what kind of programs would be fulfilling which social goals.

It would be equally important to ask why Greece—which has significant economic and political relations with neighbouring Balkan and Near Eastern countries—has a school curriculum that includes only English, French, and German as foreign languages. Why is it that the languages of its neighbors are not considered legitimate school knowledge?

Foreign Languages in Schools and Europe's Linguistic Future

Foreign language education is inevitably linked to a complex network of sociopolitical and cultural relations. However, foreign language planning has conveniently been connected to a technicist, value-free neutrality, and foreign language pedagogy has been construed as an ideologically neutral task, intended to ensure social mobility and satisfactory employment. This view is convenient for and is therefore facilitated by those who have vested interests in exporting their languages, since the exportation of a language certainly involves the exportation of particular forms of culture and knowledge.

Undoubtedly, the internationalization of a language entails economic and political advantages. No wonder that scholars who politicize issues related to language have often referred to "language internationalization" as a depoliticized term for "linguistic imperialism."[27] By this they mean using language as a means to subordinate groups in order to achieve cultural, political, and economic domination, and to regulate various domains of information and knowledge.[28] Indeed, linguistic domination simultaneously entails cultural supremacy. Those who are able to gain control over meanings and conventions of discourse are also able to promote their views of the world, their norms, their values, and ultimately their interests. Those who are denied the right to use their language in all forms of social life are hindered in expressing themselves, in shaping reality, in drawing attention to their needs, and in commanding support from others. In the final analysis, language rights reflect ideological control and power relations between social and ethnic groups within and across national boundaries.

Therefore, questions about languages in school curricula cannot possibly be examined in a vacuum. They have to be examined in their sociopolitical context, and the discursive practices of foreign language planning have to be analyzed in the context of the discourse of language planning as a whole. This is, in fact, what constitutes the central theme of this chapter. And further, we argue that the various discourses of homogenization which infiltrate the Western discourse of language planning create discursive conditions in Europe in which linguistic difference is viewed as negative and linguistic homogeneity as a key to unity.

Such views partially explain, we believe, why it is presently so difficult for the European Union to achieve its alleged desire of preserving its linguistic and cultural diversity.[29] In Western discourses, heterogeneity of any sort has rarely been construed as positive, and its potentially constructive role in sustaining social harmony has frequently been underestimated. Moreover, the aforementioned views explain the paradox of national curricula decisions regarding foreign languages to be taught in the schools of the European Union's Periphery. Here, Periphery refers to member states with low economic and political power, struggling for equal linguistic and cultural rights and yet planning foreign language education in a way that helps sustain linguistic hegemony. In the Periphery only the dominant languages are included in state school curricula, and English has a particularly prominent role to play. The nondominant languages are either partially or totally excluded. The decision to reject these languages as legitimate objects of study in schools sets the scene for the Union's linguistic future, since it results in their devaluation as economic and social assets, and in further cultural and political disempowerment of the communities where the languages are spoken. In countries which stand to gain a respectable share in the distribution of linguistic and cultural power in the Union by empowering their languages, foreign language planning promotes instead what has been referred to as "the diffusion-of-English" paradigm."[30]

To change this state of affairs the European Union must try to create conditions for the development of respect towards each society's linguistic and cultural wealth and thus avoid conflict that would ultimately endanger its unity. Europe as a suprastate and each of its members separately should reconsider issues related to language(s), language education, and language planning. A critique of the discursive practices which impede conditions for a truly plurilingual supranational state is a crucial step in this direction.[31] The next step is to develop systematically a counter-discourse at whose heart will be a truly social conception of communication—a necessary step if we are to achieve a much broader aim of redefining foreign language pedagogical practices to serve intercultural and interlinguistic goals.

The work of Gunther Kress is of particular interest to the degree that he has been articulating a social semiotic account which "recognizes that questions can be posed in different ways, through the materially differing means of (the multimodal phenomenon of) language."[32] Kress's concerns could be viewed within the framework of a postmodern project that could be understood as an attempt to retheorize the nature of language as a system of signs structured in the infinite play of difference. This would undermine the dominant, positivist notion of language either as a genetic code structured in performance or simply as a linguistic, transparent medium for transmitting preconceived ideas and culturally limited meanings and values.

Counter to this positivistic notion of language, views of language—traced to Derrida, Foucault, Jacques Lacan,[33] and Ernesto Laclau and Chantal Mouffe,[34] who have played a major role in retheorizing the relationship between discourse, power, and difference—suggest that meaning is the product of a language constructed out of and subject to the endless play of differences between signifiers. The meaning of the signifier is defined by the shifting, changing relations of difference that characterize the referential play of language.

The "borders" of language have to be opened up in our postmodern age, since the domestic and national boundaries that once held back diversity have broken down and the "receptacular imaginary" has given way to "flows."[35] Geographic, cultural, and ethnic borders have been replaced by shifting configurations of power, community, space, and time in Europe and elsewhere. This new condition of European and world order requires that we rethink and redefine the whole project of school education and of language education, in particular. We should reconsider it not merely in terms of language inclusion or exclusion from the school curriculum. We should rethink it in terms of how language pedagogy can be redefined as a form of cultural politics that will allow learners to speak in dialogical contexts which affirm, interrogate, and extend their understanding of themselves and the global contexts in which they live.

III
THE COLONIALISM OF ENGLISH-ONLY

⊸

So, if you want to really hurt me,
talk badly about my language.

Gloria Anzaldúa, *Borderlands*[1]

BOTH THE RAPID SPREAD OF ENGLISH WORLDWIDE AND THE RECENT
movements within the United States to outlaw instruction in
languages other than English should be analyzed in tandem with
a variety of contemporary race-related issues: vicious attacks on
people of color, the demonization of immigrants, the dismantling of affirmative action, and the assault on welfare programs
for the poor. These are all part and parcel of an unapologetic
dominant ideology which was unleashed with the imposition of
neoliberalism. This ideology opposes all public institutions, particularly those that are perceived to serve mostly the poor and people
of color. For example, public education in urban areas of the
United States that serves mostly nonwhite and poor students is
under siege, and public housing is struggling to survive its so-
called reform.

Interestingly enough, when publicly funded programs are used
to strengthen the dominant sphere, we hear little protest from
those media, politicians, and political pundits who otherwise
work zealously to "end welfare as we know it." These conservatives take great pride in excoriating welfare mothers for cheating

and not working, as proof of social-program abuse. Yet they remain silent about rampant fraud within the military-industrial complex, such as Pentagon payments of $700 for a toilet seat or $350 for a screwdriver. The same silence surrounded the Savings and Loan scandal, which cost taxpayers over $250 billion in welfare for the rich. In this case, the cultural commissars found it convenient to embrace public spending as a means to socialize private financial losses, yet they pontificate about the importance of privatizing social security and hold the poor responsible for creating a "social catastrophe," as Patrick Buchanan put it. Buchanan blames the "Great Society programs not only for financial losses but also for drops in high-school test scores, drug problems, and . . . a generation of children and youth with no fathers, no faith, and no dreams other than the lure of the streets."[2] However, we hear not even a peep from Buchanan and other conservative commissars decrying the unmeasurable crimes committed by Enron, Worldcom, Zerox, and other corporations that blatantly engaged in fraudulent practices and deprived millions of working people of their hard-earned retirement funds, while a handful of corporate executives walked away with billions of dollars. Some estimates have put the value of present corporate fraud at close to a trillion dollars. In essence, the scope of the current fraud perpetrated by corporations is obscene. Yet the outcry among politicians and political pundits is negligible compared to the invective these same pundits use against the poor on welfare, who, they assert, are cheating honest, hardworking taxpayers. New corporate crimes are unveiled almost on a daily basis, and the list of corporations committing high-level crimes increases, causing the stock market to plunge. Yet President Bush and his conservative cohorts continue to pursue privatizing social security because, they claim, the private sector is more efficient and is guided by the accountability of the market.

Given this landscape of selective assaults on public institutions, the bilingual education movement could not escape the wrath of the purveyors of the dominant ideology.[3] The present attack on bilingual education should not be understood as a simple critique of teaching methodologies. First, and foremost, the assault on bilingual education is fundamentally political. The denial of the political nature of the debate in itself constitutes a political action. It is both academically dishonest and misleading to point out the failures of bilingual education without examining the general failure of public education in major urban areas, where minority student dropout rates range from 50 to 65 percent in the Boston public schools to over 70 percent in larger metropolitan areas like New York City.

While conservative educators have been very vocal in their attempts to abolish bilingual education because of its putative lack of academic success, these same educators have remained conspicuously silent about the well-documented failure of foreign language education in the United States. Despite its shortcomings, no one is advocating closing down foreign language departments in schools. Paradoxically, although bilingual programs have much greater success in producing fully bilingual speakers, the same educators who propose dismantling bilingual education reiterate their support of foreign language education for the specific purpose of developing bilingualism.

The English-only movement's agenda in the United States points to a pedagogy of exclusion which views the learning of English as education in itself. What its proponents fail to question is by whom and under what conditions English will be taught. For example, in Massachusetts, a grandfather clause in the legislation governing programs for English as a second language allowed ESL teaching by untrained music, art, and social-science teachers. Immersing non–English-speaking students in these ESL programs will do very little to accomplish the goals of the English-only movement. In addition, the proponents of English-only fail to address two fundamental questions: First, if English is the most effective educational language, how can we explain that over 60 million Americans are illiterate or functionally illiterate? Second, if education in English-only can guarantee linguistic minorities a better future, as educators like William Bennett promise, why do the majority of African-Americans, whose ancestors have spoken English for over two hundred years, find themselves still relegated to the ghettos?

In this chapter we will argue that the answer to these questions has nothing to do with whether English is a more viable language of instruction or whether it promises non-English-speaking students full participation both in school and in society at large. Framing the issue in that way points to an assumption that English is, in fact, a superior language and that we live in a classless, race-blind society. We want to propose that the attempt to institute proper and effective methods of educating non-English-speaking students cannot be reduced simply to issues of language. Rather, it must rest on a full understanding of the ideological elements that generate and sustain linguistic, cultural, and racial discrimination, and which, in our view, represent vestiges of a colonial legacy in our democracy.

English-Only as a Form of Colonialism

Many educators will object to the term "colonialism" to characterize the current attack on bilingual education by conservative as well as many liberal educators. Some liberals who support bilingual education will go to great lengths to oppose our characterization of English-only movements as a form of colonialism, insisting that most educators who do not support bilingual education are just ignorant and need to be educated. This is tantamount to saying that racists do not really hate people of color; they are just ignorant. While one could argue that they *are* ignorant, one has to realize that ignorance is never innocent and is always shaped by a particular ideological predisposition. Furthermore, the attack on bilingual education or a racist act stemming from ignorance does not make the victims of these acts feel any better about their victimization.

The apologetic stance of some liberals concerning the so-called ignorance of those educators who blindly oppose bilingual education is not surprising, since classical liberalism, as a school of thought and as an ideology, always prioritizes the right to private property, while relegating human freedom and other rights to mere "epiphenomena or derivatives.[4] A rigorous analysis of thinkers such as Thomas Hobbes and John Locke will clearly show that the real essence of liberalism is the right to own property. The right to private property could only be preserved through the reproduction of a capitalist ideology. This led Liubomir Tadic to pose the following question: "Isn't conservatism a more determinant characteristic of liberalism than the tendency toward freedom?"[5] He concluded that owing to this insipid ambiguity, liberalism is always positioned ideologically between revolution and reaction. In other words, liberalism vacillates between two opposing poles. It is this position of vacillation that propels many liberals to support bilingual education, while at the same time objecting to the linkage between the attack on bilingual education and colonial language policies.

Any colonized person who has experienced firsthand the discriminatory language policies of European colonialism can readily see many similarities between colonial ideology and the dominant values that inform the American English-only movement. Colonialism imposes "distinction" as an ideological yardstick against which all other cultural values are measured, including language. In the United States this ideological yardstick serves to over-celebrate the dominant group's language to the point of mystification—viewing English as education in itself and measuring the success of bilingual programs only in terms of success in English acquisition. On the other hand, it devalues the other languages spoken by an ever-increasing number of students now populating most urban public schools. The position of U.S. English-only proponents is not very different, for example, from that of European colonizers who tried to eradicate the use of African languages in institutional life and who inculcated Africans with myths and beliefs concerning the savage nature of their cultures through educational systems which used only European languages.

If we analyze closely the ideology that informs both the present debate over bilingual education—spearheaded by the U.S. English-only movement—and the present polemic over Western heritage versus multiculturalism, we can begin to understand that the ideological principles which sustain those debates are consonant with the structures and mechanisms of colonial ideology, as succinctly described by Geraldo Davilla:

> Culturally, colonialism has adopted a negation to the [native culture's] symbolic systems [including the native language], forgetting or undervaluing them even when they manifest themselves in action. This way, the eradication of the past and the idealization and the desire to relive the cultural heritage of colonial societies constitute a situation and a system of ideas which, along with other elements, situate the colonial society as a class.[6]

If it were not for the colonial legacy, how could we explain U.S. educational policies in the Philippines and Puerto Rico? English was imposed as the only language of instruction in the Philippines, and the imposed American textbook presented American culture not only as superior, but as a "model par excellence for the Philippine society."[7] The impact of this type of mis-education is evident, for instance, in the following letter from T. H. Pardo de Tavera, an early collaborator with U.S. colonialism, to General Douglas MacArthur:

> After peace is established all our efforts will be directed to Americanizing ourselves, to caus[ing] knowledge of the En-

glish language to be extended and generalized in the Philippines, in order that through its agency we may adopt its principles, its political customs, and its peculiar civilization, [and] that our redemption may be complete and radical.[8]

The United States hoped to achieve the same "complete and radical" redemption in Puerto Rico. In 1905 Theodore Roosevelt's Commissioner of Education in Puerto Rico, Rolland P. Faulkner, mandated that instruction in public schools be conducted in English in order to make Puerto Rican schools

agencies of Americanization in the entire country ... where [schools] would present the American ideal to our youth. Children born under the American flag and on American soil should have constantly present this ideal, so that they can feel proud of their citizenship and of the flag that represents the true symbol of liberty.[9]

By leaving the colonial legacy unexamined, the purported choice to adopt an effective methodology where students are at the same time denied the opportunity to study their language and culture is, for all practical purposes, a choiceless choice. Instead of becoming enslaved by the management discourse of the present bilingual educational reforms proposed by the English-only advocates, which enhance the economic interests of the reformers while securing their privileged social and cultural positions, educators need to reconnect with the historical past so as to understand the colonial legacy that undermines American democratic aspirations. Although Renato Constantino is writing about the colonial legacy in the Philippines, his thoughtful words are both a propos and illuminating regarding our present historical juncture in education.

We see our present with as little understanding as we view our past because aspects of the past which could illumine the present have been concealed from us. This concealment has been effected by a systemic process of mis-education characterized by a thoroughgoing inculcation of colonial values and attitudes—a process which could not have been so effective had we not been denied access to the truth and to part of our written history. As a consequence, we have become a people without a sense of history. We accept the present as given, bereft of historicity. Because we have so little comprehension of our past, we have no appreciation of its meaningful interrelation with the present.[10]

Scientism as Neocolonialism

Throughout history oppressive dominant ideologies have resorted to science as a mechanism to rationalize crimes against humanity, ranging from slavery to genocide. Science is used to target race and other ethnic and cultural traits as markers that license all forms of dehumanization. If we did not suffer from historical amnesia, we would easily understand the ideology that informed Hans Eysenck's psychological proposal suggesting that "there might be a partly genetic reason for the differences in I. Q. between black and white people."[11] The same historical amnesia keeps us disconnected from dangerous memories of Arthur Jensen's racist proposals published decades ago by the Harvard Educational Review.[12]

One could argue that the above-cited incidents belong to the dusty archives of earlier generations, but we do not believe we have learned a great deal from historically dangerous memories. Consider American society's almost total embrace of scientism as exemplified by the success of *The Bell Curve,* by Charles Murray and former Harvard Professor Richard J. Hernstein. The same blind acceptance of "naïve" empiricism provides fuel to the English-only movement as it attempts to ban bilingual education in the United States. Ironically, when empirical data are provided to demonstrate that bilingual education is an effective approach for educating non-English-speaking students—as in the research of Zeynep Beykont, Virginia Collier, Kenji Hakuta, David Ramirez, and Jim Cummins, among others[13]—the data are either ignored or buried in endless debates over research design which often miss a fundamental point: the inequities and racism that inform and shape most bilingual programs.

By and large the present debate over bilingual education is informed by positivistic and management models which hide their ideologies behind a demand for objectivity, hard data, and scientific rigor. This can be seen, for example, in comments Pepi Leistyna received on a term paper on the political nature of bilingual education during his doctoral studies at the Harvard Graduate School of Education. "These are unsupported, politically motivated claims!" the professor wrote, and he suggested "a more linguistic analysis."[14] As Leistyna recounts, this same professor told him, "I hope you have been reading some hard science." This call for hard science in the social sciences represents a process through which naïve empiricists hide their anti-intellectual posture. However, this posture is manifested either through censorship of certain bodies of knowledge or through the disarticulation between theories of the discipline and empirically driven, self-contained studies. This empiricism enables the pseudoscientists to

> not challenge the territorialization of university intellectual activity or in any way risk undermining the status and core beliefs of their fields. The difference [for scientists] is that this blindness or reluctance often contradicts the intellectual imperatives of the very theories they espouse. Indeed, only a theorized discipline can be an effective site for general social critique—that is, a discipline actively engaged in self-criticism, a discipline that is a locus for struggle, a discipline that renews and revises its awareness of its history, a discipline that

inquires into its differential relations with other academic fields, and a discipline that examines its place in the social formation and is willing to adapt its writing practices to suit different social functions.[15]

As these theoretical requirements make abundantly clear, when Pepi Leistyna's professor arrogantly dismissed Freire's social critical theories, she unveiled the ideology behind the prescription that Leistyna should have been "reading some hard science." The censorship of political analysis in the current debate over bilingual education exposes the almost illusory and schizophrenic nature of educational practice, in which "the object of interpretation and the content of the interpretive discourse are considered appropriate subjects for discussion and scrutiny, but the interests of the interpreter and the discipline and society he or she serves are not."[16]

The disarticulation between the interpretive discourse and the interests of the interpreter is often hidden in the deceptive call for an objectivity that denies the dialectal relationship between subjectivity and objectivity. The call for objectivity is deeply ingrained in a positivistic method of inquiry. In effect, this has resulted in an epistemological stance in which scientism and methodological refinement are celebrated. As suggested by Henry Giroux, "theory and knowledge are subordinated to the imperatives of efficiency and technical mastery, and history is reduced to a minor footnote in the priorities of 'empirical' scientific inquiry."[17]

The blind celebration of empiricism has created a culture, particularly in schools of education, in which pseudoscientists who engage in a form of naive empiricism believe "that facts are not human statements about the world but aspects of the world itself,"[18] according to Michael Schudson.

This view [is] insensitive to the ways in which the "world" is something people construct by the active play of their minds and by their acceptance of conventional—not necessarily "true"—ways of seeing and talking. Philosophy, the history of science, psychoanalysis, and the social sciences have taken great pains to demonstrate that human beings are cultural animals who know and see and hear the world through socially constructed filters.[19]

These socially constructed filters were evident when California voters passed a referendum banning bilingual education. While school administrators and politicians were gearing up to disband bilingual programs, data from both the San Francisco and San José school systems showed that bilingual graduates were outperforming their English-speaking counterparts.[20] This revelation was met with total silence from the media, the proponents of English–only, and the political pundits. This is where the call for objectivity and scientific rigor is subverted by the weight of its own ideology.

What these educators do not realize is that there is a large body of critical literature that interrogates the very nature of what they consider research. Critical writers such as Donna Haraway,[21] Linda Brodkey, Roger Fowler, and Greg Myers, among others, have painstakingly demonstrated the erroneous nature of the claim to "scientific" objectivity which permeates all forms of empirical work in social sciences. According to Linda Brodkey, "Scientific objectivity has too often and for too long been used as an excuse to ignore a social and, hence, political practice in which women and people of color, among others, are dismissed as legitimate subjects of research."[22] The blind belief in objectivity provides pseudoscientists with a safe haven from which they can attempt to prevent the emergence of counter-discourses that interrogate "the hegemony of positivism and empiricism."[23] It is also a practice that generates a form of folk theory concerning objectivity believed only by non-scientists. In other words, as Linda Brodkey so eloquently puts it, "Any and all knowledge, including that arrived at empirically, is necessarily partial, that is, both an incomplete and an interested account of whatever is envisioned."[24] In fact, what these pseudoscientists consider research, that is, work based on quantitative evaluation results, can never escape the social construction that generates these models of analysis—models whose theoretical concepts are always shaped by the pragmatics of the society that devised these evaluation models in the first place.[25] That is, if the results that are presented as facts were originally determined by a particular ideology, these facts cannot in themselves illuminate issues that lie outside the ideological construction of these facts to begin with.[26] We would warn educators that these evaluation models can provide answers that are correct but nevertheless without truth. If a study concludes that African-American students perform way below white mainstream students in reading, it may be correct, but the conclusion tells us very little about the material conditions under which African-American students work in the struggle against racism, educational tracking, and the systematic negation and devaluation of their histories. We would propose that the correct conclusion rests in a full understanding of the ideological elements that generate and sustain the cruel reality of racism and economic oppression. Thus an empirical study will produce conclusions without truth if it is disarticulated from the sociocultural reality within which the subjects of the study are situated. A study designed to assess the reading achievement of children who live in squalid conditions must factor in the reality these children face, as described, for instance, by Jonathan Kozol:

> Crack-cocaine addiction and the intravenous use of heroin, which children I have met here call "the needle drug," are woven into the texture of existence in Mott Haven. Nearly 4,000 heroin injectors, many of whom are HIV-infected, live here. Virtually every child at St. Ann's knows someone, a relative or neighbor, who has died of AIDS, and most children here know many others who are dying now of the disease. One quarter of the women of Mott Haven who are

tested in obstetric wards are positive for HIV. Rates of pediatric AIDS, therefore, are high.

Depression is common among children in Mott Haven. Many cry a great deal but cannot explain exactly why.

Fear and anxiety are common. Many cannot sleep.

Asthma is the most common illness among children here. Many have to struggle to take in a good deep breath. Some mothers keep oxygen tanks, which children describe as "breathing machines," next to their children's beds.

The houses in which these children live, two-thirds of which are owned by the City of New York, are often as squalid as the houses of the poorest children I have visited in rural Mississippi, but there is none of the greenness and the healing sweetness of the Mississippi countryside outside their windows, which are often barred and bolted as protection against thieves.[27]

An empirical study that neglects to incorporate into its design the cruel reality just described—and which occurs often in our supposedly classless society—will never be able to explain fully the reasons behind the poor performance of these children. Pseudoscientists will go to great lengths to prevent their research methodologies from being contaminated by the social ugliness Kozol described in order to safeguard their "objectivity" in, say, studies of underachievement among children who live in ghettos. However, the residents of these ghettos have little difficulty understanding the root causes of their misery, here described by a resident of the Mott Haven community named Maria:

If you weave enough bad things into the fibers of a person's life—sickness and filth, old mattresses and other junk thrown

in the streets, and ugly ruined things, and ruined people, a
prison here, sewage there, drug dealers here, the homeless
people over there, then give us the very worst schools anyone
could think of, hospitals that keep you waiting for ten hours,
police that don't show up when someone's dying . . . you can
guess that life will not be very nice and children will not have
much sense of being glad of who they are. Sometimes it feels
like we have been buried six feet under their perceptions.
This is what I feel they have accomplished."[28]

What Maria would probably say to researchers is that we do not
need another doctoral dissertation to state what is so obvious to
the people sentenced to live in this form of human misery. In
other words, locking children into material conditions that are
oppressive and dehumanizing invariably guarantees that they will
be academic underachievers. Once underachievement is guaranteed by these oppressive conditions, it is very easy for research
studies—which, in the name of objectivity, ignore the political and
social reality that shapes and maintains these oppressive conditions—to conclude that blacks are genetically wired to be intellec-
tually inferior to whites, as was done in *The Bell Curve* by Richard
J. Hernstein and Charles Murray.[29] Along the same lines, for example, an empirical study which concluded that children who engage in dinner conversation with their parents and siblings achieved
higher rates of success in reading would not only be academically
dishonest but also misleading to the degree that it ignored the
class and economic assumption that all children are guaranteed
daily dinners in the company of their parents and other siblings.
What generalizations could such a study make about the 12 million children who go hungry every day in the United States? What
could a study of this type say to thousands upon thousands of
children who are homeless, who do not have a table, and who
sometimes do not have food to put on the table they do not have?
A study that made such sweeping and distorted generalizations

about the role of dinner conversations in reading achievement would say little about children whose houses are without heat in the winter—houses which reach such dangerously cold conditions that a father of four children remarked, "You just cover up … and hope you wake up the next morning."[30] If the father really believed the study results, he would suggest to his children, after they had all made it through another freezing night alive, that they should have a conversation during dinner the next night since it would be helpful in their reading development—should they be lucky enough to make it through another night alive. What dinner conversation would the Haitian immigrant, Abner Louima, have with his children after being brutally sodomized with a toilet plunger by two white policemen in a New York police precinct? Would his children's reading teacher include as part of his or her literacy development some articles about the savage acts committed by the white New York policemen against their father?

These questions make it clear how distorted the results of an empirical study can be when they are disconnected from sociocultural reality. In addition, such distortion feeds into the development of stereotypes that, on the one hand, blame the victims for their own social misery and, on the other hand, rationalize the genetic inferiority hypotheses that are advanced by such pseudo-scholars as Murray and Hernstein. What empirical studies often fail to point out is how easily statistics can be used to take away the human faces of the subjects through a process that not only dehumanizes but also distorts and falsifies reality.

What educators need to understand is that they cannot isolate phoneme-grapheme awareness from factors of social class and cultural identity which ultimately shape such awareness.

Fracturing Cultural Identities

Most conservative educators as well as many liberals conveniently embrace a form of naïve empiricism. This allows them to celebrate scientism and methodological refinement, while issues of equity, class, and cultural identity, among other sociocultural factors are always relegated to the margins. While the fields of bilingual education and English as a second language have produced a barrage of studies aimed primarily at demonstrating the effectiveness of English acquisition, these research studies conspicuously fail to raise other fundamental questions. Does cultural subordination affect academic achievement? What is the correlation between social segregation and school success? What role does cultural identity among subordinated students play in linguistic resistance? Does the devaluation of students' culture and language affect reading achievement? Is class a factor in bilingual education? Do material conditions that foster human misery adversely affect academic development?

These questions are rarely addressed in naïve empirical studies that parade under the slogan of scientific 'objectivity' in order to deny the role of ideology in their work. This process serves to prevent the development of counter-discourses that interrogate these studies' major assumptions. As Paulo Freire points out, when these educators claim a scientific posture, "[they often] try to 'hide' in what [they] regard as the neutrality of scientific pursuits, indifferent to how [their] findings are used, even uninterested in considering for whom or for what interests [they] are working."[31] Because most educators, particularly in schools of education, do not conduct research in the "hard sciences," they uncritically attempt to adopt the neutrality posture in their work in the social sciences, leaving out the necessary built-in criticism, skepticism, and rigor of the hard sciences. In fact, science cannot evolve without a healthy dose of self-criticism, skepticism, and contestation. However, a discourse of critique and contestation is often viewed as contaminating "objectivity" in the social sciences and education. Instead, the pseudoscientists who uncritically embrace the mantra of scientific objectivity, usually find refuge in an ideological fog that enables educators to comfortably fragment bodies of knowledge when they conduct their research. For example, they can study children who live in Mott Haven to determine their phoneme-grapheme awareness while paying no attention to the material conditions described by Jonathan Kozol—conditions that lock children into a chain of oppressive and dehumanizing circumstances which invariably guarantee they will be academic underachievers.

By reducing the principles of reading or the acquisition of English to pure technicism (i.e. phoneme-grapheme awareness), these educators can easily disarticulate a particular form of knowledge from other bodies of knowledge, thus preventing the interrelation of information necessary to gain a more critical reading of the reality. Such disarticulation enables educators to engage in a social construction of "not seeing"—which allows them to willfully not understand that behind the empirical data there are always human faces with fractured identities, dreams, and aspirations. The fracturing of cultural identity usually leaves an indelible psychological scar experienced even by those subordinated people who seemingly have "made it" in spite of all forms of oppression. This psychological scar is painfully relived by Gloria Anzaldúa, when she writes, "El Anglo con cara de inocente nos arrancó la lengua." (The Anglo with the innocent face has yanked our tongue.) "Ahogados, escupimos el oscuro. Peleando con nuestra propia sombra el silencio nos sepulta." (Drowned, we spit darkness. Fighting with our very shadow we are buried by silence.)[32] Thus colonized cultural beings are sentenced to a silenced culture.

Fragmenting bodies of knowledge also obscures the linkages necessary for understanding that the yanking of linguistic minority students' tongues is not only undemocratic but is reminiscent of colonial policies, as, for instance, recounted by the African author Ladislaus Semali.

I first went to Iwa Primary School. Our language of education was not Kiswahili. My struggle began at a very early age, constantly trying to find parallels in my culture with what was being taught in the classroom. In school we followed the British colonial syllabus. The books we read in class had been written by Mrs. Bryce, mostly adapted and translated into Kiswahili from British curricula. We read stories and sang songs about having tea in an English garden, taking a ride on the train, sailing in the open seas, and walking the streets of town. These were unfortunately stories far removed from our life experiences. As expected, we memorized them even though they were meaningless.

By the time I was in fifth grade Swahili was no longer the medium of instruction. English had taken over and Kiswahili was only a subject taught once a week. Kichagga was not to be spoken at any time, and if caught speaking [it] we were severely punished. Thus, one of the most humiliating experiences was to be caught speaking Kichagga while still on the school grounds. The culprit was given corporal punishment—three to five strokes of the cane on the buttocks.[33]

The expression, "And then I went to school," reflects an experience common throughout the world, including First World democracies like the United States, where bilingualism and multiculturalism are under constant assault by the Western cultural commissars. Americans conveniently fall into historical amnesia by forgetting the English-language reeducation camps that were designed primarily to yank Native Americans' tongues. Native-American children were taken from their parents and sent to boarding schools whose primary purpose was to cut them off from their "primitive" languages and "savage" cultures. While we ominously forget the dehumanization of American-Indian children in the so-called boarding schools, we nevertheless proudly denounce as human rights violations the re-education schools created by Communist governments. "And then I went to school," however, is not forgotten by the American-Indian writer Joseph H. Suina.

School was a painful experience during those early years. The English language and the new set of values caused me much anxiety and embarrassment. I could not comprehend everything that was happening, but I could understand very well when I messed up or was not doing well. The negative aspect was communicated too effectively, and I became unsure of myself more and more. How I wished I could understand other things as well in school."[34]

The pain of Gloria Anzaldúa's tongue being yanked and Joseph Suina's pain and embarrassment in American schools undeniably share the common experience of colonization with African author Ngugi Wa' Thiongo, who laments the loss of the Gikuyu language in Africa.

We therefore learned to value words for their meaning and nuances. Language was not a mere string of words. It had a suggestive power well beyond the immediate and lexical meaning. Our appreciation of the suggestive, magical power of language was reinforced by the games we played with words through riddles, proverbs, transpositions of syllables, or through nonsensical but musically arranged words. So we learned the music of our language on top of the content. The language, through images and symbols, gave us a view of the world, but it had a beauty of its own. The home and the field were then our pre-primary school, but what is important for this discussion is that the language of the evening teach-ins, and the language of our work in the field were one.

And then I went to school, a colonial school, and this harmony was broken. The language of my education was no longer the language of my culture.[35]

If we analyze closely the ideology that informs both the debate over bilingual education and the polemic over the primacy
of Western heritage versus multiculturalism, we can begin to
understand that those ideological principles are consonant with
the structures and mechanisms of a colonial ideology designed
to devalue the cultural capital and values of the colonized.
It is only through a full understanding of America's colonial
legacy that we can begin to comprehend the complexity of bilingualism in the United States. For most linguistic minority speakers, bilingualism is not characterized by the ability to speak two
languages. There is a radical difference between a dominant
speaker learning a second language and a minority speaker acquiring a dominant language. While the former involves the
addition of a second language to one's linguistic repertoire, the
latter usually inflicts the experience of subordination upon the
minority speaker—both when speaking his or her native language, which is devalued by the dominant culture, and when
speaking the dominant language he or she has learned, often
under coercive conditions. The colonized context and the asymmetrical power relations with respect to language use in the
United States create, on the one hand, a form of forced bilingualism and, on the other, what Albert Memmi calls a linguistic drama.

In the colonial context, bilingualism is necessary. It is a condition for all culture, all communication and all progress. But
while the colonial bilinguist is saved from being walled in, he
suffers a cultural catastrophe which is never completely over-
come. The difference between native language and cultural
language is not peculiar to the colonized, but colonial bilingualism cannot be compared to just any linguistic dualism.
Possession of two languages is not merely a matter of having
two tools, but actually means participation in two physical
and cultural realms. Here, the two worlds symbolized and
conveyed by the two tongues are in conflict; they are those of

the colonizer and the colonized. Furthermore, the colonized's mother tongue, that which is sustained by his feelings, emotions, and dreams, that in which his tenderness and wonder are expressed, thus that which holds the greatest emotional impact, is precisely the one which is the least valued. It has no stature in the country or in the concept of peoples. If he wants to obtain a job, make a place for himself, exist in the community and the world, he must first bow to the language of his masters. In the linguistic conflict within the colonized, his mother tongue is that which is crushed. He himself sets about discarding this infirm language, hiding it from the sight of strangers. In short, colonial bilingualism is neither a purely bilingual situation, in which an indigenous tongue coexists with a purist's language (both belonging to the same world of feeling), nor a simple polyglot richness benefiting from an extra but relatively neuter alphabet; it is a linguistic drama. [36]

Empirical studies that neglect to investigate this linguistic drama fully and that treat bilingualism as mere communication in two languages, invariably end up reproducing those ideological elements characteristic of communication between colonizer and colonized. These naïve empirical studies cannot but recycle old assumptions and values regarding the meaning and usefulness of the students' native languages in education. The notion that education of linguistic minority students is solely a matter of learning standard English still informs the vast majority of bilingual programs and manifests its logic in the renewed emphasis on technical reading and writing skills. For the education of linguistic minority students to become meaningful, it has to be situated within a theory of cultural production and viewed as an integral part of the way in which people produce, transform, and reproduce meaning. Bilingual education, in this sense, must be seen as a medium that constitutes and affirms the historical and existential moments of lived culture. Hence, it is an eminently political phenomenon, and it cannot be disarticulated from the very politics that shapes and maintains its implementation. Bilingual education programs in the United States in fact exist within a neocolonial educational model. By not basing bilingual education on a cultural production model, educators have created programs for linguistic minority students that not only invariably impose a disguised assimilatory model, but also deny students structures through which they could obtain a truly democratic and liberating educational experience.

While the various debates over the past two decades may differ in some of their basic assumptions about the education of linguistic minority students, they all share one common feature—they ignore the role of language as a major force in the construction of human subjectivities. That is, they ignore the way language may either confirm or deny the life histories and experiences of the people who use it.

The pedagogical and political implications in education programs for linguistic minority students are far-reaching, yet largely ignored. These programs, for example, often disregard a fundamental principle of reading, namely, that students learn to read faster and with better comprehension when taught in their native tongue. In addition, the immediate recognition of familiar words and experiences enhances the development of a positive self-concept in children who are somewhat insecure about the status of their language and culture. For this reason, and to be consistent with the goal of constructing a democratic society free from vestiges of oppression, a bilingual education program should be rooted in the cultural capital of subordinate groups and have as its point of departure their own languages.

Educators must develop radical pedagogical approaches that provide students with the opportunity to use their own reality as a basis for literacy, including, obviously, the language they bring to the classroom. To do otherwise is to deny linguistic minority students the rights that lie at the core of the notion of a democratic education. The failure to base literacy programs on the minority students' languages means that the opposing forces can neutralize the efforts of educators and political leaders to achieve de-colonization of schooling. It is of tantamount importance in the education of linguistic minority students that the minority language be incorporated as the primary language of instruction, since it is through their own language that the students will be able to reconstruct their history and their culture.

Proponents of English only and other educators who are willing to violate linguistic minority students' democratic rights to be educated in their own language as well as in English work primarily to preserve a social (dis)order, which, according to Jean Paul Sartre, "sanctions misery, chronic hunger, ignorance, or, in general, subhumanity." Educators who refuse to transform the ugliness of human misery, social injustices, and inequalities invariably become educators who, as Sartre so poignantly suggested, "will change nothing and will serve no one, but will succeed only in finding moral comfort in malaise."[37]

Conclusion

During a conference in which Donaldo Macedo attempted to unmask the ideological mechanisms involved in the present assault on bilingual education, a woman approached him and said, "Thank you very much for your courage to say things that many of us are too afraid to say." Since he was taken by surprise, he did not know how to respond, but he managed to make a point with the following question: Isn't it ironic that in a democracy, to speak the truth, at least one's own truth, one must have courage to do so? She squeezed his hand and politely said goodbye. After she left Macedo began to think that what he should have told her is that to advocate for the democratic rights of bilingual students and to denounce the inequities and the racism that shape their mis-education, "it is not necessary to be courageous; it is enough to be honest."[38] And being honest would require that we denounce those reactionary educators who believe that bilingual education "is highly contentious and politicized . . . and [that] there is a lack of clear consensus about the advantages and disadvantages of academic instruction in the primary language in contrast to early and intensive exposure to English."[39] Being honest would also require that we denounce the research industry that makes a living by pointing out the "lack of clear consensus" in the bilingual debate, yet does not provide alternative pedagogies that would effectively address the specific needs of linguistic minority students. The research industry remains complicit with those same oppressive structures responsible for the poverty and human misery that characterize the lives of a large segment of linguistic minority students who go to inner-city public schools.

For instance, take research on the Head Start program, particularly bilingual Head Start. Many white Head Start researchers are rewarded by the dominant ideology for their complicity with the doctrinal system. They receive large grants to study early exposure to literacy as a compensation for the poverty and savage inequalities with which many of the researchers remain in total complicity. Often, these studies end up stating the obvious, pointing out the proverbial "lack of clear consensus," which, in turn, calls for more research. While the call for more research ultimately benefits the researchers themselves, it invariably takes away precious resources that could be spent to diminish the adverse consequences of the inequities that inform the lives of most minority children. Being honest would require that reactionary educators acknowledge the existence of the intimate interrelationship between society's discriminatory practices and the savage inequalities that shape the mis-education of linguistic minority students. This would, no doubt, point to the political nature of education, whose recognition reactionary educators call "politicizing" education.

Accusations of "politicizing" education become a means to muffle rigorous academic debate concerning both the grievances and the educational needs of linguistic minority students. Addressing those needs requires a thorough deconstruction of the ideology that prevents linguistic minority students' sociocultural reality from becoming an area of serious inquiry. Only such an analysis could convince educators who want to take politics out of education that it is erroneous to think that "[s]peaking a nonstandard variety of English can impede the easy acquisition of English literacy by introducing greater deviations in the representation of sounds, making it hard to develop sound-symbol links."[40] This position makes the assumption that standard dialects are monolithic and show no phonological variations, and that they therefore restrict "deviations in the representation of sounds, making it [easier] to develop sound-symbol links." Such a posture is sustained solely by a folk theory that is believed only by non-linguists. Anyone who has been exposed to the Boston dialect notices that its speakers almost always drop the phoneme /r/ in the final position, as in car. Yet middle-class speakers of this dialect have little difficulty linking the dropped phoneme /r/ to its respective graphemic representation. The persistence of this folk theory can be attributed to the present excess of positivism, which elevates numbers to an almost mythical status, yet dismisses other fundamental factors that have important pedagogical implications. Consider Celia T. Leyva's account:

> Growing up, I was often reprimanded for speaking Spanish in class and even in the lunch room, and also discriminated against because I spoke English with a Cuban accent. I was ridiculed not only by classmates, but also by my teachers who insisted that I had to speak English like Americans do. Because of the humiliation I went through growing up, I felt the need to prevent my own children from similar situations,

and robbed them of the opportunity to learn my native language, and, at the same time, denied them their own culture. I hated English and I hated learning it.[41]

Perhaps factors such as linguistic and cultural resistance play a greater role in the acquisition of standard English than the mere ability to link sound and symbol. bell hooks painfully acknowledges that most African-Americans view standard English, not as a neutral tool of communication, but as the "oppressor's language, [which] has the potential to disempower those of us who are just learning to speak, who are just learning to claim language as a place where we make ourselves subject."[42] In learning the "oppressor's language," students are often forced to experience subordination when speaking it. Upon reflection, bell hooks states, "It is not the English language that hurts me, but what the oppressors do with it, how they shape it to become a territory that limits and defines, how they make it a weapon that can shame, humiliate, colonize."[43] The shame, humiliation, and colonization that non-speakers of standard English feel in their relationship with English have a great deal more to do with their lack of success in reading English than the mechanical difficulties of making sense of sound-symbol link—even those difficulties due to the unavoidable phonological variations found in all dialects, including the dominant standard English. The nature of the nonstandard dialect is not the determining factor in the subordinate students' inability to learn the ABCs, even though that inability makes it appear that they need to be taught "how to learn." These students have little difficulty learning what the chief of psychiatry at the San Diego Children's Hospital rightly described as the "more relevant skills of the DBSs (drive-by-shootings)."[44] These and other survival skills are vividly and painfully mastered by any student whose reality is characterized by violence, human misery, and despair.

Being honest would require that we reconnect with history so as to learn from the thousands of Chicano high-school students who, in 1968, walked out of their schools as a protest against their mis-education. They walked out to demand quality education, cultural dignity, and an end to cultural violence. The passion, courage, and determination those Chicano students demonstrated will serve us as a model as we attempt to refigure how to best educate linguistic minority students. Their courage, passion, and determination energized educators, political leaders, and community activists, who coalesced to address the urgent needs of Chicanos and other linguistic minority students. The needs of linguistic minority students are perhaps even greater today, given the added vicious assault on bilingual education. For this reason teachers, parents, researchers, and community members need to work together with the same determination, not only to provide quality education to linguistic minority students, but also to dismantle the social and cultural fabric that informs, shapes, and reproduces the despair of poverty, fatalism, and hopelessness.

By incorporating minority students' cultural and linguistic forms into their textual, social, and political analysis, educators will develop the means to counter the dominant attempt to impose English as the only educational practice. They will also equip themselves with the necessary tools to embrace a pedagogy of hope based on cultural production, in which specific groups of people produce, mediate, and confirm the mutual ideological elements that emerge from and affirm their cultural experiences. These elements include, obviously, the languages through which these experiences are reflected and refracted. Only through experiences that are rooted in the interests of individual and collective self-determination can we create democratic education. Cultural production, not reproduction by imposing English, is the only means through which we can achieve a true cultural democracy. In this sense, bilingual education offers us not only a great opportunity to democratize our schools, but, as Paulo Freire said, "is itself a utopian pedagogy."

It is full of hope, for to be utopian is not to be merely idealistic or impractical, but rather to engage in denunciation and annunciation. Our pedagogy cannot do without a vision of the man [and woman] of the world. It formulates a scientific humanist conception that finds its expression in a dialogical praxis in which the teachers and learners together, in the act of analyzing a dehumanizing reality, denounce it while announcing its transformation in the name of the liberation of man [and woman]."[45]

IV
LINGUORACISM IN EUROPEAN
FOREIGN LANGUAGE EDUCATION
DISCOURSE[1]

꘠

AT THIS MOMENT IN WORLD HISTORY, THE POSTMODERN PROJECT
CLAIMS the end of ideology and with it the end of geographic
inequalities and of class, race, and gender struggles as we have
known them. At this historical moment, identity politics—based
on New Individualism—characterizes freedom in terms of individual expression and preferences, leaving capitalism, sexism, and
racism intact.[2] It is a time when diversity and difference are no
longer ignored in the dominant cultural apparatus, but also a
time when practices of "Othering" are recurring. However, due
to economic and political interests, these practices seem to be
more subtle and indirect than before, as critical analysis of various social discourses consistently reveals.[3]

The Othering practices that remain relatively unchanged concern language. Discrimination in terms of the language(s) one
speaks is usually overt, and language-related prejudices are a
consistent feature of everyday talk. Representations of certain
languages in positive and of others in negative terms are facilitated through academic and professional discourses on language.

These practices are common even in the European Union, which has recently declared its commitment to respecting the linguistic rights of its member states and presumably tries to promote egalitarian language policies. Understanding how these practices occur in the discursive field of foreign language education— where particular representations of languages, language knowledge, and linguistic diversity are created—seems pertinent, since the development of a multilingual/multicultural ethos of communication is becoming an increasingly necessary prerequisite for the political unification of Europe.

Concepts for the Investigation of Evaluative Language-Related Practices

One useful concept in the literature concerned with linguistic human rights is *linguicism,* as discussed by Tove Skutnabb-Kangas and Robert Phillipson. Linguicism has to do with "ideologies and structures used to legitimate, effectuate, and reproduce an unequal division of power and resources (both material and nonmaterial) between groups which are defined on the basis of language (i.e. their mother tongue)."[4] According to Phillipson, linguicism is an "ideological construct [that] essentially involves the dominant group/language presenting an idealized image of itself, stigmatizing the dominated group/language, and rationalizing the relationship between the two, always to the advantage of the dominant group/language." Arguing that "the structures and ideologies of linguicism can best be identified and documented by placing them in an explicit theory of linguistic imperialism," Phillipson seems to view linguicism in terms of a binary opposition between the dominators and the dominated. Studies documenting linguicism, he rightly observes, may serve as a springboard "to obtain more justice for dominated languages."

The concept of linguicism is extremely useful when analyzing hegemonic operations in foreign language education planning.

When the Center, serving its sociopolitical and economic interests, constructs the superiority of its languages and language teaching practices as natural, there are processes at work that repress opposition and resistance by subordinating the Periphery. These processes reconstruct the naturalized reality concerning the so-called international languages and contribute to the unequal distribution of linguistic and cultural power. It is important, however, to focus on language-related practices that do not specifically develop in a context of linguistic/cultural imperialism, but originate in discourses shaped as a form of power that circulates in the social field.[5] These practices are in line with other forms and expressions of cultural racism and suggest that we need a concept other than that of linguicism in order to investigate them. Instead of linguicism, we suggest that *linguoracism* more accurately names the insidious racism involved in all forms of linguistic imperialism.

Linguoracism in discursive practices is realized partly by representing cultural inheritance as resembling biological inheritance.[6] Cultural systems, including language, are associated with racial collectives, as commonly expressed in utterances such as "Greek is the language of the Hellenic race." Yet, the literature devoted to the investigation of racist practices often excludes language from its agenda. While recognizing that language viewed as discourse is the basic means through which racism is shaped and maintained, discussions of the elusive term "race" do not explicitly include language as a distinguishing feature of its social construction.[7] Indeed, in some cases it is not. In German legal documents, for example, the German race is constructed on the basis of *jus sanguinis,* whereby "Germanness" is said to be transmitted from generation to generation not through language and culture but through "blood" or DNA. In other cases, however, representations of racial "identity" are strongly linked to linguistic and cultural activity. We therefore suggest that investigation of racist practices should not exclude language-related prejudices shaped and maintained in social discourses.

The coining of the term linguoracism here begs an explanation that is situated in discourse—understood after Foucault as a system of knowledge immersed in the operations of social power.[8] Linguoracism can be seen as materially developing in discursive practices that constitute the articulation of knowledge (and hence ideology) rooted in power relations. These practices emerge as specific representations of language-related reality employed by either "strong" or "weak" social, ethnic, and cultural groups—positions which are defined and redefined during the course of sociopolitical interaction. Such a conceptualization of linguoracism may help us identify language-related discursive practices that can attach to strategies of both domination and resistance. Moreover, it allows us to investigate social and disciplinary discourses that produce truth claims about the nature and use of language(s) as well as about linguistic diversity. Last but not least, this conceptualization of linguoracism helps us focus on a variety of different functions that are performed. One of these functions is the (re)production of positive and negative representations and valuations of either one's own or another language or of regional and social varieties of language (always in relation to other languages or varieties). Another basic function is the (re)production of positive and negative representations and valuations of culturally related communicative action and cultural production.

Linguoracism, like other types of racism, involves an evaluative ranking with respect to the discontinuity, particularly though not exclusively, between ethnic, cultural, and racial collectives. This is because racism is essentially hierarchical, i.e., it involves evaluation of difference in terms of inherent better or worse, higher or lower, acceptable or objectionable, and so on. Moreover, there seems to be a hierarchy among groups practicing racism. This is what Teun van Dijk implies when he argues that both popular and elite racism exist but that the former derives from interpretation of the discourse of the latter.[9] However, whereas racism and other related "isms" (such as sexism, elitism, and so on) have often developed on panethnic or nonethnic foundations, linguoracism is ethnically and culturally related. Therefore, it entails discursive practices that first construe some languages and communicative behaviors (not necessarily one's own) as superior to all others and then assert that linguistic and cultural purity are a prerequisite for the development and even survival of a culture. Linguistic hybridity, pluralism, and difference are portrayed as dangerous.

Linguoracist Practices

The teaching of language and linguistics positions teachers and researchers in a fertile laboratory to collect data concerning students' discursive practices as articulations of the social and disciplinary knowledge they have been developing. Instances of linguoracism, such as the following comments written by a male student in his sociolinguistics exam paper, are not uncommon.

Allowing the citizens of a country to speak another language is dangerous. Language is what helps people keep their national and cultural roots. If they are allowed to use a second language, there is a great danger that they might forget who they are, what the history of their nation is.

Such truth claims could be situated in the social networks of power relations between ethnic and cultural communities, revealing the antagonisms and synagonisms embedded in discourses which construe ethnic and cultural purity in positive terms. They are based on representations of language as both a "mirror" and a "creator" of culture and nation. As such, linguoracism is articulated by ethnic groups whether they are politically, economically, and culturally powerful or powerless. Instances of linguoracist practices by ethnic minorities in social settings where they experience linguistic and cultural domination are indeed quite common—because of this domination but also regardless of it.

The primary aim of this chapter is to problematize foreign language education discourse along these lines and to bring in examples of the aforementioned discursive practices. It will become clear that linguoracism is not the prerogative of the dominating stratum. This chapter draws information from the reports of a research project presently being carried out in Britain by a team of Greek linguists and educators. The aim of this project is to provide suitable criteria for reforming curricula, syllabi, and teaching materials used in Greek language education programs intended primarily for the children of Greek and Cypriot immigrants to Britain.[10] So far, the project team has been evaluating the Greek language program by reviewing syllabi and materials, as well as questionnaire and interview responses by students, teachers, parents, and Greek community school administrators. The discursive practices of everyone (including the students) are striking expressions of linguoracism, which is also occasionally present in the texts of the project team that reports their findings. The Greek language is represented as the "mother" of all European languages and the Greek civilization as the cornerstone of Western civilization. The purpose of teaching Greek is "to preserve Hellenism in the psyche of the Greek 'homogeneia'"—"homogeneia" (ομογένεια) meaning a group of people from the same race, as the word "genos" (γένος) translates into "race." In evaluating the curricula and syllabi of the Greek language schools, it is striking that they do not focus on the communicative and cultural experiences of the students, nor on topics and skills that are part of the students' daily lives. The schools are set up by the Greek community with significant support from the Greek Orthodox Archidice and are staffed with personnel provided by the Greek and Cypriot states. The Greek language programs in these schools are actually designed to acculturate youngsters so that they are not assimilated into the dominant culture. It is interesting that the two cultures are viewed in oppositional terms within the framework of cultural relations between the Greek minority and the dominant British majority.

Linguoracism and European Discourses of Homogenization

Linguoracism seems to be contingent on the European discourses of homogeneity that contributed to a monolingual ethos of communication, which is very different from the multilingual ethos of India, for example, as described by Lachman Khubchandani.[11] This monolingual ethos is articulated in the discourses of the academic disciplines of theoretical linguistics, sociolinguistics and language planning, education, and curriculum theory through discursive practices regarding language and language use. It is important to review briefly how the discourses of these disciplines separately and together have construed ethnic, cultural, and linguistic homogeneity as positive and pluralism as negative. We believe that their truth claims have infiltrated foreign language education discourse and resulted in linguoracist practices.

Let us start by referring to the discipline of language planning. A critical study of the field's discourse reveals that its basic function has been to describe in apolitical terms the role that government-authorized activity has played in solving the "problem" of plurilingualism/culturalism created by the great shifts of population in Europe. The construction of plurilingualism/culturalism as a problem is related to 1) European claims that a single language is the very basis upon which ethnic consciousness and identity are formed, and 2) the idea that borders of states conform politically to linguistic boundaries. As Norman Fairclough points out:

The notion of a language, as it grew in Europe, was tied to the growth of nation-states and their perceived need to strengthen their hold over diverse groups of people by developing the concept of a homogeneous ethnicity. It was this need which gave birth to the fundamentally important notion of a single language as a shared means of communication between a homogeneous national/cultural group.[12]

As James Tollefson has argued, the discipline of language planning legitimated such claims and hence the power of the state to make language a mechanism for the expression of nationalism and a means to manipulate feelings of security and belonging.[13] Discursive practices in early works on language planning represent linguistic homogeneity as the basic characteristic of states that are "economically more developed, educationally more advanced, politically more modernized and ideologically-politically more tranquil and stable."[14] And even though it is increasingly clear that a state policy imposing a shared language in multilingual societies is often accompanied by social division rather than integration, language planning discourse continues to present as somehow irrational any resistance to the process of unification through one language or one language variety.[15]

Even a superficial analysis of the discourses of other language-related disciplines reveals a process of legitimizing the homogeneity ideals that resulted from very particular political and cultural circumstances in Europe.[16] The basic paradigm in theoretical linguistics, for example, systematically represents language as a self-contained, fixed system, amenable to an analysis which excludes the social, cultural, and political implications of language acquisition and use. It thus helps to normalize monolingualism and social homophony. Sociolinguistics, on the other hand, largely legitimates the "language-equals-ethnicity/culture" norm. Analyzing the discourse of texts adopting an ethnography of speaking methodology, for example, reveals consistent representations of ethnolinguistic homogeneity. When we critically analyze comparative and contrastive studies of speech, such as those by Shoshana Blum-Kulka and Elite Olshtain, Maria Sifianou, and Deborah Tannen,[17] among many others, we see that they view culture as a collectivist phenomenon which explains the totality of belief and behavior of individuals as members of a cultural group. At the other end of the line is the work of linguists such as Emanuel Schegloff[18] and Robert Hopper,[19] who insist on investigating communicative behavior patterns in universalist terms. They view communicative actors, not as social subjects with culturally defined identities, but as autonomous interlocutors who conform to universally devised communicative rules.

Foreign Language Education and Linguoracism

Western homogenization discourses are very evident in foreign and second language education practices. Second language teaching in schools, which is said to provide "equal opportunities" for upward mobility to the young of minority groups, has actually aimed at the assimilation of students into the dominant culture. Such is the case, for example, in the enterprise to teach English as a second language (ESL) in Britain and the United States. ESL education in these two countries can be seen as linguoracism in action. There are even a few scholars and educators, like M. Syer and Maurice Mullard, who discuss ESL as a racist act. Speaking of British education, Syer notes, "It brands some children (almost inevitably black) as having problems which would have been avoided had they not had the impertinence to come here in the first place." He understands that the cause of the problem is not the language deficiency the students experience, but the emphasis the British educational system places on one language, namely English. Mullard, on the other hand, who also questions the motives behind ESL, points out that the aim of ESL education and accompanying programs of cultural indoctrination and subordination is to neutralize subcultural affinities and influences within the school.[20] Such efforts, which usually fail to provide the opportunities they promise, often result in equally linguoracist practices on the part of minority groups, who either reproduce the discourses of the dominant culture by which they have been absorbed or, in developing oppositional consciousness, articulate discourses of resistance.

Critiques of language education practices in member states of the European Union other than Britain indicate varying degrees of linguoracism. Some of those states, which are also characterized by linguistic and cultural diversity, have developed linguistic and cultural integration programs for the children of minority groups and/or have provided opportunities for these youngsters to receive instruction in their mother tongue, at least during the years of basic education. A case in point is Germany, which provides opportunities for Danish and Serbian children to access knowledge during their basic education in their "first" language. Other minorities, including children of Turkish, Kurdish, and Italian immigrants, are branded in official documents as "foreign children."[21] These children are offered "support programs" so that ultimately they learn German, which is said to be the "normal" language of formal education, and so that they obtain German school qualifications. In Sweden children of the Sami population have the choice of attending a state-run Sami school, while Swedish as a second language is offered in all Swedish schools.[22] All schools also make available the four dominant foreign languages (English is compulsory) as well as "home" languages, i.e., the languages spoken in the homes of, say, Finnish and Portuguese immigrants. This state of affairs differs considerably from that in the European states that until recently were either characterized by relative linguistic and cultural uniformity or represented themselves as linguistically and culturally uniform. In Greece, for example, state schools generally do not offer Greek as a second language for the children of older or recent immigrant populations. Moreover, Greek is the exclusive medium of instruction, and schools do not provide support programs to help the children of minority groups become integrated without becoming assimilated. Finally, they do not offer a foreign language curriculum that includes languages other than the three dominant European languages. English is compulsory during basic education, and French and German are offered in secondary education.

Specific questions about language in the school curriculum are indeed politically sensitive issues—questions such as how the official/national language is offered in schools, whether it is also offered as a second or as a foreign language, how and which other languages are included or excluded from the school curriculum. These are often answered by linguoracist practices in varying degrees. By and large, these practices have developed as part of the discourse of homogeneity in the discipline of educational curriculum theory.

Curriculum planning in Western societies has generally aimed at the production of subjects with a national identity. The social role of the curriculum has been to develop a high degree of normative and cognitive consensus among the heterogeneous elements of society, so that they can finally be embraced as part of the narrative of the national culture without disturbing its norms. In fact, the underlying assumption on which curriculum design has often been based is that recognition of difference can constitute a threat to the values, customs, and traditions of a society. Therefore, the discursive practices of curriculum planning do not represent difference as productive nor the dynamics of change as natural and normal. Linguistic differences and other cultural and social differences are considered largely to be potentially subversive factors, rather than conditions upon which to build the curriculum. This becomes evident in Clark's work, which reviews the basic trends in curriculum design and the educational value systems underlying them. Clark has been concerned with curriculum development specifically for foreign language teaching.

Clark sees three prevalent modes of curriculum design, which evolved from past to present on the basis of different educational value systems. He describes the three categories as follows: 1) Classical humanism is elitist, concerned with generalizable intellectual capacities and with the transmission of knowledge, culture, and standards from one generation to another. 2) Reconstructionism is concerned with bringing about social change through the educational system, with achieving a social consensus on common goals, and with planning rigorously to achieve them. 3) Progressivism is concerned with the development of the individual as a whole person, with personal and group responsibility, with promoting natural learning processes through various stages of development, and with fostering a capacity for learning how to learn.[23]

Clark's critical reading of these systems indicates that they express visions of the person "as a whole," with either generalizable or with individual innate intellectual capacities. Society is construed as a unified entity with "common goals." It is seen as a body of objectively definable knowledge and a set of universal standards which each culture, as a finite, self-sufficient unit, can transmit. Society is understood not as people's lived experiences but as a set of normative, consensually shared principles.

It is interesting also to review the modes of curricula to which, according to Clark, the above educational value systems give rise. 1) Classical humanism gives rise to a content-driven curriculum, in which the subject matter is analyzed into elements of knowledge which are then sequenced from simple to complex. Classes are set up or streamed and moved as a block through units of work. Assessment is norm-referenced and concerned with the selection of an elite for the next stage of education. 2) Reconstructionism gives rise to a goal-driven curriculum, in which the content is derived from an analysis of the learner's objective needs in terms of behavior. Content is sequenced from part-skills to whole-skills and from simple to complex. The methodology lays stress on part-skill practice, the rehearsal of goals, and the mastery of predetermined criteria. Assessment is criterion-referenced and concerned to show what learners have mastered and at what levels. 3) Progressivism gives rise to a process-driven curriculum, governed by principles of procedure designed to allow learners to negotiate goals, content, and methods.[24] Learning is experiential. Learners are expected to impose their own order on what is learned. Assessment is concerned with both process and product, and is negotiated with individuals.

A critical examination of the above modes of curriculum design reveals a glaring absence of concern with difference. First of all, they ignore social difference as a relational concept, stemming from cultural markers such as social class, gender, race, and ethnicity. They also neglect the more inert inventory of unrelated diversity which stems from disembedded social identities and intercultural and interlingual subjectivities. On the contrary, what is strikingly present are concerns with knowledge seen as objective, neutral, and value-free.

Issues that politicize knowledge have remained outside the mainstream discourse of curriculum theory. Curriculum design has been concerned primarily with achievement and learning, and theoretical considerations have resulted in discursive practices about a mere "how to." All this is directly relevant to the choice of foreign languages and to the type of foreign language education offered in schools. Issues about *what language knowledge counts as legitimate, whose language is important enough to be included in the curriculum, why, and in what terms* have usually not been reviewed in terms of the linguoracism that choices of foreign language and foreign language pedagogy entail. Yet, the choices of European schools in their articulations as homogenizing discourses have developed in apolitical terms to construct specific social meanings and reproduce linguoracist practices, since they systematically represent some languages and cultures as more important than others.

This has been the main principle upon which foreign language education in Europe has been based. Foreign languages have been a traditional part of the official knowledge provided by modern schools in the West, and decisions about the inclusion or exclusion of languages in the curriculum were the result of commonsense attitudes stemming from Eurocentric ideals. The political agenda behind such decisions remained hidden. Thus ancient Greek and Latin were considered a necessary part of elite education to provide the youth of privileged classes with "real" culture. In addition, one or more modern European languages of international prestige were made available to youngsters, since their acquisition was viewed as important for the cultivation of the mind and for the development of poise and character. Linguoracist practices represented individuals who did not know French or German, for example, as only partially educated and therefore justly excluded from the circles of the social elite and the intelligentsia. Demands for knowledge of the "important" European languages were greater on native speakers of the "weak" languages, because knowledge and use of the former were supposed to give them access to the achievements considered of intellectual and cultural value. Hence, foreign language education, an essential part of meritorious education in Europe, was a linguoracist enterprise, finding expression in classroom practices and in the way foreign language programs, syllabuses, and materials were designed.

In the postwar period and in this new age of pragmatism, foreign language education has acquired new social meanings. As the teaching and learning of foreign languages has aimed explicitly at making possible urgently needed international communication, foreign language education implicitly has been granted a substantial commercial and political role. This role can best be enacted by promoting languages that profitably represent political, cultural, and economic power. English, the language of commerce and technology, is the number one global choice, while French and German are choice number two in Europe, with Spanish racing but still well behind. Therefore, although the European Union proposes teaching all European languages, foreign language teaching in European schools is still synonymous with dominant language teaching. The "weak" languages of Europe are often totally excluded and when included are attributed little or no significance in European curricula.

The unequal distribution of linguistic power in Europe is sustained not only by systematically including some languages and excluding others, but also by including certain languages that the system does not promote. Greek, for example, is included in the national British curriculum,[25] which also offers the rest of the E.U. languages, plus Arabic, Bengali, Chinese (Cantonese or Mandarin), Gujarati, Hebrew, Hindi, Japanese, Punjabi, Russian, Turkish, and Urdu, all in a unified language curriculum.[26] Nevertheless, the Greek project group that was referred to earlier reports that not many schools offer Greek language classes because the Greek state does not provide teachers and their salaries—at least not as frequently as the Turkish state does! The variety of social meanings in this double practice are interesting. We are referring first to the act of British authorities, whose refusal to provide adequate funds for the teaching of a "weak" language such as Greek, precludes the actualization of a choice that is provided on paper only. We also refer to the act of the antagonistic representation of this condition on the part of the Greek project group in reference to Turkish. If we review this particular practice within the framework of the British national curriculum's topic-based syllabus for all foreign languages, including the so-called "community languages," we become aware of the linguoracism it articulates.

A critical analysis of the text of the 1991 British document regarding modern foreign languages in the national curriculum may lead to other interesting observations and perhaps the conclusion that the unequal distribution of linguistic power is sustained through the language programs developed. One may note, for example, that content organization is an exclusive expression of social experiences in Western culture to which all minority groups must be assimilated. Tuku Mukherjee is one of few educators who make a critique of the program for teaching non-Western languages in Britain.[27] He suggests that in this instance it is not ESL but the minority pupils' first languages that are used to acculturate them into the national culture. Practices which can be viewed as acts of resistance on the part of the minority groups often are as linguoracist as the practices of the dominant group, if we consider the Greek community school example.

The social meanings articulated when British and other European schools offer the dominant languages are different. These programs seem to aim at making students familiar with the foreign culture so that they develop expert linguistic performance and native-like communicative competence. Communicative approaches for the teaching of "strong" languages, developed within the framework of "innovative" foreign language education theories, entail teaching methodologies and techniques through which students are supposed to learn to use the language correctly and also appropriately. What this boils down to is that learners are to develop the necessary sociocultural skills to accommodate native speakers of the target culture. Learners are expected to acquire the communicative skills needed to apologize, categorize, discriminate, ask for directions, and give instructions in ways appropriate in the target culture, to initiate and close a personal or formal letter or report, to give the weather forecast, or produce an ad in accordance with target sociocultural practices. In fact, pragmalinguistic and sociopragmatic "infelicities" are the object of systematic investigation in a whole area of study concerned with contrastive pragmatics in foreign language teaching and learning.[28] These infelicities are measured against native-speaker norms even when a foreign language program aims at teaching a particular language as a contact language between native speakers of languages other than the one being taught. Given that the languages considered a necessary part of official school knowledge in Europe are by and large the dominant languages, foreign language teaching methods have aimed at acculturation processes. However, the reverse is true when and if the "weak" languages are offered.

Linguoracist practices which legitimate this state of affairs are produced not only by those interested in sustaining linguistic and cultural power, but also by those who are concerned with their language rights and otherwise struggle for an equal share in the distribution of linguistic power. The reasons for this ostensible paradox can certainly be traced to structural conditions and hegemonization processes which should not be underestimated. However, it is important that they should also be traced to the European homogenizing discourses. In deconstructing them, we hope to denaturalize the commonsense meanings they have construed. In genealogizing them, we hope to develop new discourses that represent difference and diversification as positive. On the basis of this knowledge, multilingualism and multiculturalism may be understood as options to be pursued.

The European Union has stated its commitment to preserving its multilingual and multicultural nature. Yet, it seems to be facing a problem resulting from what is often perceived as a conflicting aspiration. On the one hand, it aspires to achieve political and hence cultural integration, and on the other, it wants to maintain its linguistic and thus cultural diversity. It is contented that the two aims do not conflict with one another. These aims seem to conflict because Europe's discursive formations of integration are situated in its homogenization discourses—discourses which facilitate the articulation of linguoracist practices.

Conclusion

The first step in the direction of change from linguoracist to linguofair practices requires a critique of the discourses that impede conditions for plurilingualism. This has been one of the objectives of this chapter. Our future goal is to contribute to the development of a counter-discourse, at the heart of which will be a truly social conception of language that will help us redefine foreign language pedagogical practices to serve intercultural and interlinguistic goals.

To develop a discourse that represents linguistic diversity as productive, we must turn to the work of those theorists who have been attempting to re-theorize the nature of language as a system of signs structured in the infinite play of difference. These theorists undermine the dominant, positivist notion of language as either a genetic code structured in performance or simply as a linguistic, transparent medium for transmitting preconceived ideas and culturally limited meanings and values. Theorists such as Jacques Derrida, Michel Foucault, Jacques Lacan, and Ernesto Laclau and Chantal Mouffe move their discussions beyond the technicist and reductionistic view of language as an apolitical and neutral tool of communication equally available to all speakers.[29] The so-called neutrality of language not only hides the ideological context that permeates language but also serves as a mechanism to reproduce the dominant social order.

In the present multicultural and multilingual twenty-first century, when borders are collapsing with magical speed, it is of paramount importance that foreign language programs cease to colonize through their purported language neutrality. The new conditions of this new world order require that we refigure what it means to teach a foreign language so that it becomes a process to include rather than exclude the Other.

This redefinition should not be made merely in terms of language inclusion or exclusion from the school curriculum. We should rethink how language pedagogy will allow learners to speak in dialogical contexts that affirm, interrogate, and extend their understanding of themselves and the multicultural/multilingual contexts in which they live. A counter-discourse of foreign language education has to abide by principles of interculturalism and interlingualism. It must articulate new goals in language curricula that will produce differently conceived syllabuses and new approaches and methods in foreign language teaching and learning. It must facilitate new subjectivities for learners and develop new discourses based on diversity and respect for difference—linguistic or otherwise.

V
RECLAIMING THE LANGUAGE OF POSSIBILITY: BEYOND THE CYNICISM OF NEOLIBERALISM

I happen to believe that questions are hardly ever wrong; it is the answers that might be so. I also believe, though, that refraining from questioning is the worst answer of all.

Zygmunt Bauman, *In Search of Politics*[1]

IN THE PRECEDING CHAPTERS WE ATTEMPTED TO UNVEIL THE IDEOL-
OGY behind the present hegemony of English and its implications for education, language planning, and cultural autonomy.
In this chapter, we argue that beyond the importance of understanding how other national languages are steadily losing ground
to English in important political and economic spheres of communication, it is of paramount value to analyze the language of
neoliberal ideology—an ideology which permeates, in a stealth-
like manner, even those national languages of countries that
have bravely resisted the domination of English within their
national boundaries. Ironically, the same ideology that has cata-
pulted English into its present hegemonic state has found widespread acceptance, at least among the dominant sectors, in
societies that correctly fight for linguist sovereignty. In other
words, while many nation-states denounce the imposition of
English upon their civic, cultural, and institutional life, they
blindly embrace the very language of neoliberalism that under-

girds the ideology behind the present worldwide hegemony of English.

There is much talk currently on different crises that American society is facing: the crisis of values, the crisis of the economy, the crisis of politics, the crisis of youth, the crisis of democracy, and the crisis of the public, among others. The use of the word "crisis" in these discourses points to a sense of loss or absence, an upcoming nihilism, or a notion of cynicism that, in turn, creates a sense of fatalism and brings about a closure. Crisis in the aforementioned examples calls for a *telos* that would neatly "arrange" all the problems and "close the case." This view of crisis has manifested itself through conservative works of neoliberal utopianism that profess the "end of ideology," the "end of history," the "end of racism," or the "end of politics."[2] However, "crisis" by definition implies an opening up of possibilities and meanings. As Cornelius Castoriadis suggests, borrowing a concept from Hippocrates, a "crisis" is a moment of decision. As a medical term, the crisis of an illness is the paroxysmal moment that will result either in the death of the patient or the beginning of the healing process, due to a beneficial reaction produced by the very crisis.[3] Within this framework, in a given crisis, not only is there an opening of possibilities, but there are also opposing elements that struggle with each other. However, what characterizes our contemporary societies is the increasing "disappearance of social and political conflicts."[4] In other words, we are not witnessing a real crisis to the extent that a crisis would signify a rupture in institutions and meanings or the opening up of questions for an ongoing dialogue. On the contrary, what we are witnessing is a hypnosis of dissident discourses, a "crisis of critique," that is, a degradation, trivialization, and closure of meanings that shut down any and all questions. At the same time, the very language is being redefined to serve an operationalist role designed to suffocate dissent and to assume a strictly functional process of endorsing the dominant market discourse. We use the term "neoliberalism" to refer to the economic, political, and cultural practices that give primacy to the market order where profit and consumption are the defining factors of any reality.

Against this neoliberal backdrop, instead of having choices that would multiply conditions for constructive debate we are witnessing a "crisis of critique" and a closure of language meanings that are symptomatic of a deeper generalized crisis in political culture, society, and democracy. Hence, the debate should necessarily be positioned and understood within the framework of advanced capitalism and the current neoliberal (dis)order. These factors not only trivialize and distort public discourses as part of their depoliticizing function,[5] but they also generate and legitimize their own "transparent" and "natural" discourse that serves as a vehicle for circulating their myths and ideologies. In this process, linguistic mediations are lost and, according to Herbert Marcuse, language "tends to express and promote the immediate identification of reason and fact, truth and established truth, essence and existence, the thing and its function."[6] The current "crisis of critique" signals the cessation of questioning and the suffocation of critique. This general failure to question is a direct by-product of the neoliberal ideology, which has managed to produce a powerful myth about itself that it does not need to be interrogated. It has acquired, in a sense, the symbolic power to transcend history in that it has brought closure to the most pressing questions of our times. Neoliberal politics pretends to provide the answers for concepts and ideas that should remain perpetually open and be constantly questioned and redefined if they are to contribute to a vital political culture and a process of democratization. Nothing is more threatening to a democracy and the political existence of its citizens than the illusion that all questions have been answered, that there are no meanings to struggle over, that there is no need for meaning mediation because words are transparent and speak for themselves. If neoliberalism has managed in part to achieve that level of "transparence," "naturalness," and "inevitability," it has done that through a powerful discourse of "universality" and "Truth." As Zygmunt Bauman has observed, "[w]hat ... makes the neoliberal worldview sharply different from other ideologies—indeed, a phenomenon of a separate class—is precisely the absence of questioning, its surrender to what is seen as the implacable and irreversible logic of social reality."[7]

In an era of triumphant neoliberalism, the strictly imposed corporate language works not only to reflect the prevailing market order and its ideologies, but also to produce a positivistic discourse that obliterates public concerns about the social and the political. In other words, as Marcuse has noted, "[t]he functionalization of language expresses an abridgement of meaning which has a political connotation. The names of things are not only 'indicative of their manner of functioning,' but their (actual) manner of functioning also defines and 'closes' the meaning of the thing, excluding other manners of functioning."[8] This closure of meaning points to a gradual extinction of language as a means of making sense of the world, or as a public good, inextricably connected to human agency, identity, and political existence. The obliteration of new possibilities in meanings and the imposition of a dominant norm for both producing and understanding language cannot be understood outside the reigning positivism and rationality in advanced capitalist industrialized societies, where "the market mechanism is the sole director of the fate of human beings and their natural environment."[9]

The triumph of positivism and rationality in neoliberal discourse is nowhere more obvious than in the appropriation and redefinition by the capitalist market ideology of concepts such as "freedom," "democracy," and "community," among others. These terms should serve as both requirements and tools to human agency, involving, according to Larry Grossberg "relations of participation and access, the possibilities of moving into particular sites of activity and power, and of belonging to them in such a way as to be able to enact their powers."[10] Instead, they are trivialized in an economic jargon that uses them and celebrates them in order to maintain and serve its own world order and ideological purposes. What follows is an analysis of neoliberalism's language and the effects it has in limiting public participation in a democratic society. In particular, we will consider how language works to disconnect effects from corporate policies, how it universalizes the market in ways that make it seem natural and self-evident, and finally, how it creates an illusion that a multiplicity of choices exist that are open to everybody.

At this juncture, the commodified language becomes both the tool and the end of neoliberal ideologies that operate in order to "guarantee" their aggressive practices. Their effects include the erasure of the welfare state, the shrinking of the public sector, the transfer of public wealth to private hands, and the minimalization of the functions of the state, a process that jeopardizes its civilizing and helping functions.[11] Neoliberalism imposes a logic whereby the state gives up its social functions to undertake a surveillance and policing role, a logic that suggests "a borderless world not for labor, but for capital."[12] Against this landscape, we provide a discussion about how it would be possible to reclaim a decommodified language, a language *of* and *for* the social, a political language that would serve as both a means and a requirement of human agency and of individual and collective autonomy.

The Functions of Neoliberalism

To allow the market mechanism to be sole director of the fate of human beings and their natural environment ... would result in the demolition of society.... Robbed of the protective covering of cultural institutions, human beings would perish from the effects of social ex-

posure; they would die as the victims of acute social dis-
location through vice, perversion, crime and starvation.
Karl Polanyi, *The Great Transformation*[13]

In 1944 Karl Polanyi made the above prophetic statement in his
book, *The Great Transformation*. Unfortunately, over fifty-five
years after Polanyi's insightful remarks, the reality attests to the
truth of his statement. We are currently witnessing the domination of a market economy that has, in turn, generated a "market
society." Within this new market society, the functions of the
state have been largely redefined, the public good has been
replaced by consumer goods, the social has no language to be
discussed, and the political is increasingly becoming depoliticized. Politics is becoming more and more irrelevant to people's
lives, and it has been reduced to the act of voting every four
years. According to Castoriadis, we are witnessing in the occi-
dental world "a type of individual that is not anymore the type
of individual of the democratic society or of a society where we
can struggle for more freedom, but rather a type of individual
who is privatized, who is closed into his/her small personal
milieu and who has become cynical regarding politics."[14] Neoliberal practices have drained politics of its vitality and force, turn-
ing it into "a metaphor for the entrepreneurial self as the
determined, autonomous subject who is able to put his or her
practices into effect."[15] Henry Giroux's work is instrumental at
this point, especially his claim that what is lost in this perspective
are "important questions about the varied sites, practices, and
forms of power that give meaning to how politics is shaped,
deployed, and played out on a daily basis." He concludes along
these lines that "politics imitates the market to the degree that
it highlights the importance of struggle but ignores the ethical
implications of such struggles."[16]

Within the confines of a market-driven politics, the market
itself becomes tautonymous to democracy, embracing a "conver-

gence dogma" whereby market and democracy converge. This becomes succinctly clear in the dominant discourse of U.S. foreign policy. Generally, freedom is evoked when issues of trade and markets are invoked. We hear terms such as "free trade" and "free market" when discussing the democratization of a given country, but human rights and social justice, which should be at the center of any democratic proposal, are often relegated to the margins. The discourse around human rights is used only as a cover to penetrate other countries' economies and/or to legitimize military interventions abroad. The United States has made capitalism into an exportable good, a commodity labeled "democratization," and it has been trying to export it all around the world. However, democracy cannot be exported. It is both a regime and a process intimately tied to specific cultural, political, and historical conditions, and it should necessarily be instituted by and for the people. The notion of "exporting democracy" becomes just another ideological trick to veil the imposition of the neoliberal order and the quest for new markets. Thus, democracy is usually understood as being synonymous with the opening up of markets and with the removal of government constraints. Absent from this "market democracy" is any discussion that would unveil the deeply political character of the markets. However, as Colin Leys states, "Contrary to the impression given by neoliberal ideology and neoclassical economics textbooks, markets are not impersonal or impartial but highly political."[17] Markets are systems of rules and regulations that are linked in complex ways to other markets, and they are embedded directly or indirectly in a vast range of other social relations that are inherently unstable.

Acknowledging the market's political character would allow us to talk about the effects and consequences that this politics has on real people's lives. A case in point is the recent bankruptcy of Kmart, the nation's third largest discount retailer. The media coverage only addressed the corporate money loss, focused on Kmart's competition with the rival WalMart chain, and analyzed ways the corporation could be revitalized. While Kmart was filing for bankruptcy (or "reorganization," as they euphemistically call it on their corporate website), the former CEO and chairman was leaving with $9 million in his pocket. (Kmart got $2 billion from a federal judge in new financing to pay employees and restock the shelves.) Unfortunately, in order to "reorganize" this badly administered, bankrupt business, the company had to close down 320 stores and lay off 22,000 workers—the third-largest layoff in the retail industry since Sears, Roebuck & Co. laid off 50,000 workers in January 1993. Layoffs (also referred to as downsizing) translate into people losing their jobs, and that is inextricably related to housing, food, health insurance, and so forth. The TV networks certainly did not broadcast profiles of the workers that became unemployed. They did dedicate a great deal of time to talking about the CEOs and the public-relations people, as if the 22,000 employees were invisible. What was more important in the public discourse was that the closings would free up about $550 billion in cash for Kmart to use to revamp existing stores, as if Kmart as a corporate entity was in more need than the people who made it work. Much discussion was also dedicated to the services and products of the Kmart chain, as well as the role of Martha Stewart, the queen of home products, in revitalizing Kmart culture. There was little possibility that the former Kmart CEO would starve from hunger—the average corporate CEO in the United States was paid as much as 42 factory workers in 1980, 122 factory workers in 1989, and 209 factory workers in 1996.[18] Absent from this discourse was the fate of the people working in the 320 Kmart stores that were closing down. These were most likely people who worked for minimum wage and supported families of three or more.[19] What kind of impact did the layoffs have on their lives? How was their health insurance affected (if they had any)? What about their housing situations? Their daily meals? Their kids' education? And this happened in a country where after massive layoffs and union-busting, less than 15 percent of workers are unionized. Neoliberal discourse erases the issues just as it depoliticizes the conditions that produce them.

Another example of how language works to disconnect corporate policies from their effects is the coverage of a strike in New England at the Interstate Bakery Corp., famous for producing the popular Twinkies. According to the local TV network's three-minute report on the issue (called "an obscure labor dispute" by the Boston Globe[20]), employees in the factory were going on strike, and the problem that emerged was that consumers were going to be deprived of their favorite snacks. The report took great pains to show footage of grocery stores where the shelves were empty of Twinkies and to interview frustrated consumers who could not believe that there were no Twinkies on the shelves. Suddenly, Twinkies became a collectible with a very important exchange value. However, what we never found out from the report was why the employees were on strike. What were their demands on the corporation that owns 53 percent of the bread market share in New England? We also never found out how the employees' demands were going to be met by the employer, nor what the outcome of the strike would mean for their wages, living conditions, and civic existence. In this case language worked to hide the true issue—the fact that the workers were struggling for their rights and had demands that would make their lives and the lives of their families better. Instead, it emphasized only the fact that a certain commodity was disappearing. People can live without some commodities or products; they cannot live without decent wages and without the solidarity of other people. When the consumer good has a higher exchange value in the politics of public discourse that the quality of human life, there is something very dangerous that threatens the roots of a so-called democracy. Language works to neutralize this danger and make it invisible.

It is necessary to make these linkages between economic events and the human consequences because there is a clear dichotomy in neoliberal ideologies between economy and policies. In other words, neoliberalism presents itself as an economic doctrine that professes free markets, deregulation, and freedom from government restrictions and trade controls, disguised under a positivistic economist discourse of "naturalness" and "inevitability." At the same time it neglects to talk about the effects of this economic theory on real people or the social costs of implementing such an economic order. This neglect has given rise to alarming poverty indices, as in the case of the total collapse of the Argentinian economy. The Argentinian middle class has practically disappeared, and over 49 percent of the population has now joined the ranks of the poor, all in the name of "freedom" and "democracy." Deriving its social force from the political and economic power of those whose interests it defends, neoliberal politics tends to favor separation between the economy and social realities. This allows those interests to construct, in reality, an economic system corresponding to Pierre Bourdieu's theoretical description of it as "a kind of logical machine, which presents itself as a chain of constraints impelling the economic agents."[21] In this way, language masks human suffering by diverting attention away from the lived experience of the people involved, directing it instead towards market causes.

The separation between the economic and the social is very much part of a neo-liberal agenda whereby increasing social inequalities, the widening gap between the rich and the poor, and human suffering are perceived as individual problems or issues of character. Discussion centers around transactions, interested parties, and agreements, or around skills, competition, and choices, and these topics are largely presented as if happening in a laboratory vacuum. Absent from this discussion are questions about who is affected by these transactions (certainly the so-called "interested parties" do not include the unemployed, welfare recipients, or people working on minimum wage), or what these transactions or policies are costing in terms of jobs, unemployment, human suffering, sickness, suicide, alcoholism, drug addiction, and so forth. By using words such as "interested parties" or "consumers," instead of "people" or maybe "citizens," neoliberalism conveniently positions subjectivities in an absolute apathy and inertia regarding any political project. Being a "consumer" already presupposes that you have a range of options and that you have the means to consume. It does not presuppose that you can question your very identity as a consumer, nor that this very identity really strips you of any form of agency that would call into question this reductionist notion of citizenship. The neoliberal "economic challenge," which supposedly invites everybody to choose from a pool of "equal opportunity," ignores the lines of class, race, gender, education, age, disabilities, and so forth. It also typecasts people as skilled or unskilled workers, educated or uneducated, successful or not successful, while it leaves unchallenged the already existing inequality inherent in the system that builds skills. It obscures the fact that choice may not be the same for people who do not have the resources to materialize these choices, in a society that largely promotes injustice and inequality of choices, opportunities, and resources.

The "crisis of critique" becomes obvious in the cases described above, where no questions are asked about the meaning of "options" and "choices," nor about the neoliberal notion of "freedom" that uses language to block important questions from being asked. For instance, what does a call for more economic freedom really mean in societies where the vast majority of people live in dire poverty? How does it affect people who do not own or manage corporations, that is, the vast majority of population? How is the inclusive "we" used in neoliberal discourse as a transparent subject that corresponds to an equal, homogeneous, and unproblematic sociohistorical entity? What are the functions of the state that neoliberalism wants to eliminate, and what is their impact on citizens? Does the elimination of these functions also apply to "corporate welfare"?

These questions need to be connected to a context where the market is expanding uncontrollably in all sectors of human life, where everything is becoming privatized, and where the state is giving up little by little its helping and welfare functions. The neoliberal demand for a minimal state threatens those civilizing and welfare functions of the state that "promote the adjustment of people to rapidly changing conditions and enable them to live together in a relatively peaceful way," or that "directly promote the well-being of people."[22] Instead, within a corporate reality, the state adopts solely a policing and surveillance role. It becomes, according to Beck, "a state that chips away at habeas corpus or trial by jury, increases prison sentences, steps up border patrols, and prepares for terrorism as the weapon of the weak."[23] For instance, according to Bourdieu, in the United States, "the state is splitting into two, with on the one hand a state which provides social guarantees, but only for the privileged, who are sufficiently well-off to provide themselves with insurance, with guarantees, and a repressive policing state for the populace."[24]

As the state is weakened in terms of its welfare functions and ceases to impose rules upon the market frenzy—not to mention corruption, as demonstrated by the collapse of Enron—its power is transferred and diffused, losing its political nature and becoming a "meta-power."[25] As a result, the state becomes depoliticized. The agenda for political choices today can hardly be politically constructed, as there is an ongoing separation of power from politics.[26] Power now has a less and less constrained mobility, is no longer geographically tied to any location, and is not contained within nation-states. On the contrary, power is extraterritorial, it flows. This extraterritorial conception reverses the logic of the traditional understanding of power, violence, and authority. Capital is exported and circulated in international markets, and, contrary to neoliberal claims that there is no source of power, capital and the market become the sole sources of power. The difference is that the locus of this power cannot necessarily be set geographically, since as Beck argues, "the economy has broken out of the cage of territorially and nationally organized power conflict and has acquired new power moves in digital space."[27] As a consequence, the market is more mobile; it is not tied to a specific geographic locus and therefore can be disposed globally as it is controlled and managed by transnational corporate powers. The extraterritoriality of power necessarily affects our understanding, as the source of decision-making and policy-implementation becomes invisible and its effects become inevitable.

The Discourse of Inevitability or the Inevitability of Discourse?

> The neo-liberal apotheosis of the market confuses *les choses de la logique avec la logique des choses,* while the great ideologies of modern times, with all their controversies, agreed on one point: that the logic of things as they are defies and contradicts what the logic of reason dictates. Ideology used to set reason *against nature*; the neo-liberal discourse disempowers reason through naturalizing it.
>
> Zygmunt Bauman, *In Search of Politics*[28]

It is neither a coincidence nor a natural phenomenon that while neoliberal policies have been directly or indirectly detrimental to the lives of millions of people, neoliberalism still remains in people's minds an important currency and a viable and "successful" doctrine, even for those who have mostly suffered the consequences of its catastrophic effects. This happens largely because neoliberal ideologies have been legitimized and disseminated

through a well-organized network of diffusion that has succeeded in presenting the neoliberal order as the inevitable effect of
an economic doctrine. This network of diffusion has functioned
to establish neoliberal ideologies along the lines of what Terry
Eagleton calls "strategies of legitimization." In this sense, the
neoliberal framework has been promoting "beliefs and values
congenial to it," and it has been naturalizing and universalizing
such beliefs, producing thus the discourse of self-evidence and
inevitability. It has been denigrating ideas that might challenge
it, and it has been excluding rival forms of thought. Finally, it
has been obscuring social reality by "suppressing social conflicts,
from which arises the conception of [neoliberal] ideology as an
imaginary resolution of real contradictions."[29]

If we take a closer look at neoliberal discourse, we will realize
that it is deeply rooted in a language of universalism and inevitability that "naturalizes" its premises. As Susan George notes,
one explanation for the triumph of neoliberalism and the economic, political, social, and ecological disasters that go with it is
that neoliberals "have created a huge international network of
foundations, institutes, research centers, publications, scholars,
writers, and public-relations hacks to develop, package, and push
their ideas and doctrine relentlessly."[30] One of the responsibilities of this network is to create a language that has the force to
justify the unjustifiable, to produce a "strong discourse" that
functions as a perfect representation of reality. George insists
that the millions of dollars spent on think tanks are not a waste,
because "they have made neoliberalism seem as if it were the
natural and normal condition of humankind. No matter how
many disasters of all kinds the neoliberal system has visibly created, no matter what financial crises it may engender, no matter
how many losers and outcasts it may create, it is still made to
seem inevitable, like an act of God, the only possible economic
and social order available to us."[31] The sense of inevitability that
characterizes neoliberal societies makes them examples par excel-

lence of "heteronomy,"—the condition where it is believed that the laws and institutions of a society have been inevitably put in place by somebody or something that lies outside the civil society. According to Castoriadis, societies should be autonomous, that is, self-instituted historically through the dynamics and politics that exist within them with the actual and active participation of people. However, in the case of heteronomy (<heteros>: different, <nomos>: law), society is seen as a creation given by somebody else: the ancestors, gods, the God, the "laws of history" (in a Marxist sense), or by capital and the markets (as is the case with neoliberalism and capitalism). The institution of society is perceived as being given by a metaphysical entity, something that exists outside civil societies, something that is "stronger" than people. Given the neoliberal political context, questioning the laws and institutions is tantamount to questioning God or some sort of established authority that is uncritically embraced by the society in question. Heteronomy obliterates questioning and dissent, because its institutions are reduced to common sense that is naturalized in people's minds. Heteronomy functions, therefore, in conditions of closure of meaning. In a capitalist reality, heteronomy functions to establish and perpetuate the myth that the market is the sole director of human societies and that it creates the institutions and the laws. This is supposedly entrenched in the "nature" of human beings, and this biological nature is seen as coinciding with an economic order. For instance, Milton Friedman's proposal is a case in point. He suggests that human freedom and economic freedom are very much part of human genetics to the extent that "we are all of us imbued with them. They are part of the very fabric of our being."[32] What is particularly insidious in Friedman's discourse is brilliantly captured by Bourdieu, who argues that "this fatalistic doctrine gives itself the air of a message of liberation, through a whole series of lexical tricks around the idea of freedom, liberation, deregulation, etc.—a whole series of euphemisms or ambiguous uses of words ... designed to present a restoration as a revolution, in a logic which is that of all conservative revolutions."[33] The euphemisms function to strip concepts like freedom, equality, community, or democracy of the very meanings that would put them at the core of a democratic and autonomous (as opposed to heteronomous) society and the exercise of human agency.

The Case of Freedom

In the culture, ideology, and politics of neoliberalism, the concept of "freedom" has a central role. According to Henry Giroux, "[f]reedom is negatively reduced to freedom from government restraint, and the rights of citizenship translate into the freedom to consume as one chooses." However, the freedom to demand free education, free housing, and free health care is met with an aggressive assault, since "[t]he state ... becomes a threat to freedom, particularly the freedom of the market, as its role as guardian of the public interests is actively disassembled, though its powers are still invoked by dominant interests to ensure their own privileges, such as free trade agreements, government subsidies for business, and strike 'negotiations.'"[34]

In order to redefine the concept of freedom, neoliberal ideologies produce a powerful discourse whose effects are so pervasive that it becomes almost impossible for anybody to even imagine freedom outside of the market order. Therefore, anybody interested in the process of the production and dissemination of such discourse should necessarily address the following questions: What is so powerful about the so-called "freedom to consume" that makes the discourse on neoliberal freedom so appealing and natural? How does neoliberal discourse manage to become so powerful as to appear inevitable? How are choices and opportunities materialized on the basis of available resources? Are the 30 million

Americans who go hungry every day really free to choose? How is it that individual and collective freedoms collapse into the freedom of the markets? Does the anthropomorphism of the "Market" (the notion that the Market has a body, character, or human qualities) make it easier for individuals to relate to it on a personal level? How can we redefine the notion of freedom as part of our human agency?

Bourdieu suggests that the current market discourse gains its strength from the fact that "that there is nothing to put forward in opposition to the neoliberal view, that it has succeeded in presenting itself as self-evident, that there is no alternative."[35] The inevitability and self-evidence of this discourse stem in part from its positivistic and rational character. As noted by Marcuse, "[t]he sentence becomes a declaration to be accepted—it repels demonstration, qualification, negation of its codified and declared meaning. ... Analytical predication of words such as freedom, democracy, equality, etc. or transgression of the discourse beyond the closed analytical structure is incorrect or propaganda."[36] In this process, the way human beings mediate meanings gets lost, and the only intelligible language becomes the language of corporations and the market, the language of advertising, or the cinematic language that becomes both the referent for clarity and the mediator between ourselves and the world of signifiers. This is largely a language stripped of nuances and closed down so that referents and signifieds can only be "observable" and "tangible." The need to talk about tangible, observable, and measurable sizes, to break down events into material segments, and the total empiricism in the analyses that are seen as ultimately leading to some sort of Truth, dominate the public discourse in an overwhelming way. These factors remind us always that "the imposing structure unites the actors and actions of violence, power, protection, and propaganda in one lightning flash. We see the man or the thing in operation and only in operation—it cannot be otherwise."[37] This "operational" strategy erases any possibility for moving beyond prepackaged meanings, for establishing a public dialogue, or for reaching a thorough understanding that would go beyond the operationalist logic.

Along these lines, freedom acquires some sort of materiality and abandons the transcendent meanings that would necessarily link it to a struggle for something that does not provide instant gratification and pleasure as commodities do. Freedom in capitalism becomes a thing, a commodity, a product. It is never questioned and, therefore, never struggled over or redefined. It exists as an entity on its own that can be owned, used, and abused. It waits to be materialized in the different manifestations and activities of capitalist life. Freedom as commodity mobilizes our desires. We want the thing, the observable tangible materiality; we dread investing in or struggling for something that is not there for our eyes to see. However, according to Benjamin Barber, "[m]arkets give us the goods but not the lives we want; prosperity for some, but despair for many and dignity for none. The consumer has an identity, but it is an identity that satisfies neither the demands of brotherhood nor the imperatives of equality and liberty."[38] Within this reductionistic context described above, freedom is understood in its Gestalt nature, as a behavior, an attitude disconnected from a broader worldview. It is the "freedom to buy something," operating in a functionalist logic and largely ignoring the ideological net around it that shapes and sustains it. As a result, it becomes a universal, it denotes a function, its transitive meaning is lost; it does not need to be problematized as it has already become common sense. It cannot go beyond descriptive reference to particular facts. It hides the linkage between the facts and the effects. However, by relegating itself to a mere descriptive reference, it becomes prescriptive.

More dangerously, this type of freedom carries a great many assumptions that almost always are left unproblematized. For instance, it presupposes an illusory variety of opportunities and choices.

This was clearly understood by Marcuse when he argued that in a highly capitalist society the only freedom remaining is the freedom to choose from preconditioned choices that often lead to a choiceless choice. According to him, "[f]ree election of masters does not abolish the masters or the slaves. Free choice among a wide variety of goods and services does not signify freedom if these goods and services sustain social controls over a life of toil and fear—that is if they sustain alienation."[39]

The illusion that there exist choices, but not *equal* choices, as the prerequisite for freedom is one of the basic premises in the work of neoliberal guru Milton Friedman. He also embraces neoliberal universalism and inevitability and claims that free markets are integral to human nature. His notion of freedom is reduced to removing tyrannical state controls. Even according to liberals such as Derek Bok, resistance to state control is intrinsic to the American character. Bok suggests that "firmly rooted in our traditions is an instinctive distaste for strong government."[40] Both Bok and Friedman allude to some sort of distorted genetics theory to explain deeply social and ideological constructions, and this is what gives to their discourse its natural character. If the desire for free markets is genetically determined and if the distaste for big government is instinctive, then who would dare question the authority of these "natural" facts?

Friedman is clear that Americans never had it so good, and that more market freedom and less state restraint are necessary conditions for prosperity and affluence. Any force to the contrary or, as Bauman points out, any attempt at self-limitation "is taken to be the first step on the road leading straight to the gulag, as if there was nothing but the choice between the market's and the government's dictatorship over needs—as if there was no room for citizenship in other form than the consumerist one."[41] Thus, the theology of freedom to consume becomes, according to Friedman, "[a]n essential part of the economic freedom [that] is freedom to choose how to use our income:

how much to spend on ourselves and on what items; how much to save and in what form; how much to give away and to whom."[42] This logic is echoed by Robert Reich when he states that "[m]ost of us are more prosperous than ever before. We own more."[43] If we look closely into these statements we can identify a common underlying assumption that often distorts reality. That "we" is an umbrella for everybody living under the reality described; "our income" is a common denominator, a referent to talk about both the few wealthy and the vast majority of the poor. One cannot help but wonder whether these people live on the same planet where "the financial wealth of the top 1 percent of U.S. households now exceeds the combined household financial wealth of the bottom 95 percent."[44] Obviously the groups situated at the two poles of this economic reality have neither the same choices nor the same resources or opportunities. Consequently, we need to adhere to Bauman's suggestion that choice involves two sets of constraints. One is the *agenda of choice*— "the range of alternatives which are actually on offer," which is necessarily linked to material conditions. The second is the *code of choosing*—"the rules that tell the individual on what ground preference should be given to some items rather than others and when to consider the choice as proper and when as inappropriate."[45] With this framework of reference in mind, next time we talk about choices we should consider the agenda of choice for the 31 million Americans—including 12 million children—who regularly go hungry or can't afford balanced meals.[46] And next time we want to talk about freedom to spend "our income," we should consider the 10 million Americans who have no bank accounts. These people pay hefty fees to cash checks or pay bills, and more important, "they are not building the credit records needed, for example, to buy a house or to secure a loan to start a business."[47] In addition, next time researchers are "puzzled why so many low-income families do not save or hold little or no assets"[48] and blame that situation on "financial illiteracy," we could point to the 5.4 million Americans who live in substandard housing and spend more than half their income on rent.[49] The agency invoked in the discourse around choice is not simply "a matter of the spatial relations of places and spaces and the distribution of people within them. ... It is a matter of the structured mobility by which people are given access to particular kinds of places (and resources), and to the paths that allow one to move to and from such places."[50]

The poverty figures speak volumes about people who cannot cover their basic vital needs, who have no income, who cannot even give a security deposit to secure an apartment, much less buy commodities, spend on leisure, or save.[51] So, while "the average size of a new home has expanded from 1,500 square feet to 2,190 square feet," according to a 1997 report of the National Coalition for the Homeless, nearly one-fifth of all homeless people (in twenty-nine cities across the nation) are employed in full- or part-time jobs.[52] Barbara Ehrenreich succinctly captured the situation:

Gail is sharing a room in a well-known downtown flophouse for $250 a week. Her roommate, a male friend, has begun hitting on her, driving her nuts, but the rent would be impossible alone.

Annette, a twenty-year-old server, who is six months pregnant and abandoned by her boyfriend, lives with her mother, a postal clerk.

Marianne, who is a breakfast server, and her boyfriend are paying $170 a week for a one-person trailer.

The other cook, Andy, lives on his dry-docked boat, which, as far as I can tell from his loving descriptions, cannot be more than twenty feet long.

Tina, another server, and her husband are paying $60 a night for a room in the Days Inn. This is because they have no car and the Days Inn is in walking distance of the Hearthside.

Joan ... lives in a van parked behind a shopping center at night and showers in Tina's motel room.[53]

Ehrenreich's testimony contradicts glaringly those who blindly embrace and promote the "freedom to choose" and the "never-had-it-better" dogma. Obviously, the people in Ehrenreich's account do not exactly have the "freedom to choose," mainly because given their material conditions, they really have no choice. Along these same lines, while "the number of cars has risen from one car for every two Americans age 16 or older to one car for each driving-age adult," and while "the number of Americans taking cruises each year has risen from 500,000 to 6.5 million and the production of recreational vehicles has soared from 3,000 to 239,000," the poverty figures are steadily increasing.[54] The same inequities apply to the issues of unemployment, drug abuse, incarceration, human suffering, lack of health insurance, and so forth. Neoliberal analyses comfortably leave out "the significant number of people living on the razor's edge, materially speaking, in the 'most affluent nation on earth'"[55] and fail to analyze why these people do not have access to opportunities and choices. In this case, the discourse around freedom uses language to perpetuate and expand the existing inequalities without challenging the underlying social structures and institutions that construct them and perpetuate them. While the contradictions in the neoliberal discourse become more and more obvious, the proponents of neoliberalism still insist that social problems are issues of character and that social concerns are private troubles. Markets promote private rather than public forms of discourse, "allowing us consumers to speak via our currencies of consumption to producers of material goods, but preventing us from speaking as citizens to one another about the social consequences of our private market choices."[56] By adopting a language that is stripped of any ethical referent, we remain consumers, largely enclosed by our own little individual worlds. This language of individualism is promoted by the "experts" who come to justify the unjustifiable, or as Marcuse would say, to prove the rationality of the irrational. The language of the "expert" is manifested in Derek Bok's claim that "any doctrine emphasizing monetary rewards and tolerating highly unequal incomes can be morally defensible only if it includes a commitment to give all citizens opportunities to compete and to progress to the full measure of their ability."[57] We do not believe that any doctrine that promotes social inequality can be morally defensible. We do, however, believe in politics rooted in ethics and justice that serves the democratic imperatives of public life. Any politics stripped of the ethics that provide "a way of recognizing a social order's obligation to future generations"[58] is a politics without a project. Unfortunately, Bok reproduces what Anatole Anton considers one of the illusions of neoliberalism—that "individuals with the same talent and abilities would be equally productive, independent of the social resources available to them and, thus, owe little to the society that provides the context for their achievements."[59] We feel that what is provocatively missing from this type of discourse is an explanation of the fact that worldwide, "three billion people presently live on $2 or less per day while 1.3 billion of those get by on $1 or less," yet "there [are] now roughly $60 trillion in securitized assets (stocks, bonds, etc.), with an estimated $90 trillion in additional assets that will become securitizable with the global reach of today's 'emerging markets' development model. With help from [its] global regulatory agent, the WTO, neoliberalism is evoking a future where a handful of the world's most well-to-do families may pocket more than 50 percent of that $90 trillion in financial wealth."[60]

Paul Street argues that in the present capitalist state of affairs people are "free to be poor" without anybody feeling the moral and ethical responsibility to intervene to change this reality.[61] According to him, while leading architects of American policy and opinion claim that people are freer than ever before and that "democracy is literally sweeping the world as the twentieth century comes to a close," the poverty rates are steadily increasing together with human misery and suffering. Child poverty (one out of four children is born into poverty), unequal distribution of wealth (the top 1 percent of families have about the same amount of wealth as the bottom 95 percent), wage rates, affordable housing, and healthcare (42 million people have no insurance while 29 million are underinsured) are the indicators that point to a different reality which is rarely taken into account when freedom is discussed in neoliberal analyses.[62]

On the contrary, freedom is often invoked in discussions about markets, trade, finance, and the act of consuming, as, for instance, when Friedman parallels voting with shopping. While he praises the freedom to elect our representatives, at the same time, he insists that the freedom to vote is

very different from the kind of freedom you have when you shop at a supermarket. When you enter the voting booth once a year, you almost always vote for a package rather than for specific items. If you are in the majority, you will at best get both the items you favored and the ones you opposed but regarded as on balance less important. Generally you end up with something different from what you thought you voted for. If you are in the minority, you must conform to the majority vote and wait for your term to come. When you vote daily in the supermarket, you get precisely what you voted for, and so does everyone else. The ballot box produces conformity without unanimity; the marketplace unanimity without conformity. That is why it is desirable to use the ballot box, so far as possible, only for those decisions where conformity is essential.[63]

Friedman's notion of democracy speaks volumes about the kind of politics that neoliberalism has put into place. It also speaks volumes about what it means to live in a society where the only form of agency available is to consume. In a society where politics is so disarticulated from public life, Friedman's language gains "naturalness" and becomes unproblematic to most people. In this state of affairs, citizens are turned into consumers or human capital, and civil societies become commercialized malls. In fact, malls, as deeply depoliticized living spaces, have not only outnumbered secondary schools and post offices, they have acquired such centrality in the new social order that entire families now go to malls instead of parks, which suffer more and more draconian cuts in their maintenance budgets. In some states, while shopping malls are proliferating, parks are either in disrepair or are being closed down.

Redefining freedom within this framework would mean not only unveiling the contradictions discussed above, but also moving towards the decommodification of both public spaces and the very language used within these spaces. It would also mean reclaiming a language *of* and *for* the social. Challenging the neoliberal notion of freedom would ultimately lead us to Bauman's brilliant remark that "all unfreedom means heteronomy." In other words, freedom is inextricably linked with the processes and functions that institute and sustain an autonomous society, where individuals, as a collectivity, participate in the creation of their own rules and institutions. This is a deeply democratic process. The opposite promotes a type of freedom that is stripped of its liberatory qualities and becomes distanced from autonomy because it serves a logic that brooks no question or dissent. This gives rise to heteronomy, where people stop asking questions about the nature of the system that is imposed on them because they begin to perceive such imposition as common sense. In this case people are mostly convinced that they do not have to fight for freedom because freedom is presented to them as a prepackaged gift. It becomes transparent and its meaning is compromised. As a result, the neoliberal notion of freedom collapses into its very "transparency," in that it is not self-explanatory nor does it point to a specific materiality or object. Freedom is not observable to the eye, nor does it have an exchange value that could be measurable in the mall of neoliberalism. Unfortunately, as Bauman suggests, "[t]he passage to the late-modern or postmodern condition has not brought more individual freedom—not in the sense of more say in the composition of the agenda of choices or more capacity for negotiating the code of choosing. It only transformed the individual from political citizen into market consumer."[64] Freedom in a democratic sense should mean transforming the consumer into a *zoon politikon,* a political being, in the Aristotelian sense.

The recontextualization of the term "freedom"—not in order to challenge, resist, or rupture, but rather to serve domination and heteronomy—is also manifested when it is repeatedly pronounced by neoliberal conservatives. Their usage reminds us that our consciences should refuse to rest easy with the disappearing meaning of freedom.[65] In other words, freedom in the neoliberal philosophy gets de-historicized and removed from its inherently oppositional and liberatory projects that should lead to both individual and collective autonomy. Therefore, one should always become suspicious when, for instance, a limitation of freedom is presented as a solution that will protect freedom. Take for example, the recent Patriot Act, which gives government officials carte blanche on surveillance of U.S. citizens, under the pretext of protecting freedom. Edward Said asserts that

> by passing the Patriot Act last November, Bush and his compliant Congress have suppressed or abrogated or abridged whole sections of the First, Fourth, Fifth and Eighth Amendments, instituted legal procedures that give individuals no recourse either to a proper defense or a fair trial, that allow secret searches, eavesdropping, detention without limit, and,

given the treatment of the prisoners at Guantanamo Bay, that allow the U.S. executive branch to abduct prisoners, detain them indefinitely, decide unilaterally whether or not they are prisoners of war and whether or not the Geneva Conventions apply to them—which is not a decision to be taken by individual countries.[66]

When the call for freedom implies more surveillance and more regulation of both public and private life, then something else is at work that rocks the very notion of freedom and democracy. At this point, and in order to understand the concept of freedom, it would be interesting to review Hannah Arendt's discussion of freedom and totalitarianism. According to her, a "totalitarian government does not just curtail liberties or abolish essential freedoms; nor does it ... succeed in eradicating the love for freedom from the hearts of men. It destroys the one essential prerequisite of all freedom, which is simply the capacity of motion which cannot exist without space."[67] She adds that implicit in the discussion of freedom is the notion of a shared space between men and women, a public space that is erased when "men [sic] are pressed against each other." Thus, totalitarianism, in order to "abolish the fences of laws between men—as tyranny does—means to take away man's liberties and destroy freedom as a living political reality; for the space between men as it is hedged in by laws is the living space of freedom."[68] In this sense, freedom becomes both a living and a political reality. Freedom would suffocate if there were not enough space, that is, it would not be able to survive outside the existence of a vibrant public sphere.

Unfortunately, in the United States public spheres have been shrinking and becoming more and more depoliticized. Public goods are currently under attack, starting with a healthcare system that is managed privately and is available only to those who can afford it. The U.S. media is dominated by fewer than ten conglomerates, whose annual sales range from $10 billion to $27 billion. These include major corporations such as Time-Warner, General Electric, Disney, Viacom, TCI, and Westinghouse.[69] The language involved in these spaces is deeply marked by a market seal. In higher education we also see a radical turn towards corporatization and privatization. Students in colleges and universities are customers, GAs and TAs are cheap labor, and tenure-track positions are becoming extinct. The mission of the university is being re-articulated in terms of the job market/ stock market, knowledge is perceived as a commodity, preference is given to knowledge that is directly applicable and marketable, and curriculum is subordinated to specific corporate needs (as a matter of fact, curriculum now pertains to the CEOs' responsibilities). Tuition has become a premium for the university's product. Friedman illustrates this situation when he claims that "the college is selling schooling and the students are buying schooling. As in most private markets, both sides have a strong incentive to serve one another. If the college doesn't provide the kind of schooling its students want, they can go elsewhere. The students want to get full value for their money."[70] Following this line of argument, Friedman proudly quotes an undergraduate student from Dartmouth College saying that "[w]hen you see each lecture costing $35 and you think of one of the other things you can be doing with the $35, you're making very sure that you're going to go to that lecture."[71] Obviously when economics take over the pedagogical, something needs to be said not only about the changing nature of educational institutions— which are now being re-articulated and restructured to function on the model of corporations—but also about the very language that is used to sustain such a model. The corporate privatization model is infiltrating every domain of our society, including prisons. As Anton points out, "[t]he increasing rate of incarceration in the United States in combination with a flat crime rate speaks to prisoners as human commodities for newly emerging private-prison companies. The punishment industry has become a booming addition to the private sector."[72]

These examples and many more point to the increasing disappearance of urban spaces where people come into contact with each other, of contemporary agoras that bring people together. The public arena, "a zone where people could enter into discourse with others, exchange ideas, mount debates, and influence collective decision-making—where, in fact, important problems of common concern could be addressed—has degenerated well beyond even those minimal standards of liberal capitalism."[73] Any discussion of freedom must invariably be connected to the extension rather than contraction of public spheres such as we are unfortunately witnessing in advanced capitalist societies. In the present cultural discourse on freedom, public spheres should be understood as open civic spaces, both ideological and material, where the free trade of ideas, knowledge, and practices takes place—a reclaimed decommodified territory where people can exercise a truly democratic citizenship. In short, public spheres should be highly political and should aim at human self-governance and at freeing people from the logic of the market. Public spheres must not be curtailed in the interest of the dominant ideology, and they must be reconceived beyond the notion of commodity. As Giroux clearly argues, "[t]he concept of public sphere reveals the degree to which culture has become a commodity to be consumed and produced as part of the logic of reification rather than in the interest of enlightenment and self-determination."[74]

The gradual collapse of the public into the private has produced a notion of freedom that is very much individualized and privatized. Notions of solidarity, collectivity, and community are losing their content under the pressure of competitiveness and success. The notion of freedom has been separated from any political project. It is becoming an empty term that not only "reflects ... control but becomes itself an instrument of control even where it does not transmit orders but information; where it demands, not obedience but choice, not submission but freedom."[75]

An Interventionist Pedagogy

> We accuse them of criminalizing the freedom to oppose. We call the people to overcome the attitudes that immobilize them. We call them to take the streets and speak out. We are millions ... and this is not their planet. Against a capitalist Europe and against war. Another world is possible!
>
> From the Manifesto read at the Barcelona demonstration against corporate Europe, March 16, 2000

Neoliberalism as an economic, political, and cultural practice has dismantled the bridges that link private to public life. Today, more than ever before, Bauman asserts, there is "no easy or obvious way to translate private worries into public issues and, conversely, to discern and pinpoint public issues in private troubles."[76] The call for more individual freedom sinks people into a more and more isolated and private life, while the collective initiative is dying and the political is reduced to the act of voting. Even voting implies an illusionary choice, since in the United States, a vocal advocate of multiparty systems, the two parties are so perfectly similar in their methods, objectives, and goals that what we truly have in place could be viewed as the most perfect one-party system in the world. Furthermore, "representatives" are also commodities to the extent that one needs more than $40 million to get elected to the U.S. Senate. Who contributes to a $40–million campaign chest? Certainly not the unemployed, low-wage workers, or welfare mothers. The commodity character of neoliberal societies has resulted in a state of "unfreedom"—a regime of heteronomy whereby laws and institutions are imposed by a market order. The economy dictates its rules to the society rather than society making the rules and conditions for the markets. However, markets are simply not designed to do the things that democratic civil societies do, and consumers will not and cannot promote civic virtue by pursuing private ends.[77]

Unfortunately, the language used in these commodified spaces is necessarily a commodified language. One way that market ideology is naturalized and disseminated is through the use of a de-historicized language, where terms such as freedom, democracy, autonomy, community, and solidarity acquire a new content and serve the logic of accumulating capital. By denuding the language that is used to legitimize the current social and political (dis)order, we can recognize "the limits and social costs of a neoliberal philosophy that reduces all relationships to the exchange of goods and money."[78] That is, by positioning language historically and looking through the projected transparency of the terms, we can re-appropriate a politicized language—a language that has a political project.

There is more at stake here than the awareness that language needs to be decommodified and that its meanings need to be ruptured so as to "break the continuity and consensus of common sense."[79] It is not enough to locate and expose the linguistic functions in communication that perpetuate market domination by neutralizing meanings. The existence of a de-commodified language does not guarantee a political project in any way. We need a new kind of literacy that moves beyond "communicative action" and "interpretive understanding." As Homi Bhabha suggests, we need a type of literacy that acts as "an equalizing force." The kind of literacy that is not merely about competence but "is about intervention—the possibility of interpretation as intervention, as interrogation, as relocation, as revision—is often not taught even at the best institutions."[80] In addition to developing a language of possibility and critique, we need to link decommodified language to a notion of human agency as the mediation between constraints and possibilities. While there is a huge communicative dimension in language, communication is hardly an end in itself, and, as Castoriadis says, "it is totally inadequate as a way of bringing out criteria for action."[81] In public discourse, "communicative action" and "interpretive understanding" are two important moments, but in no way do they define its meaning or its end. To paraphrase Castoriadis, the end of this type of intervention should not be "interpretive understanding" of the discourse so as to unveil its contradictions, but rather a contribution to people's access to their own autonomy (their capacity to challenge themselves and to lucidly transform themselves).[82] This project is fundamentally pedagogical—a project for a "paideia of autonomy" against the triumph of capitalist significations—and, therefore, also political. This pedagogical project would necessarily require a language that is open, free from operationalism and functionality, a historical language that is part of a democratic imaginary signification which questions any and all authority, including the authority of our own proper thoughts. Giroux is worth quoting at length here when he suggests that

[c]hallenging neoliberalism also demands new forms of social citizenship and civic education that have a purchase on people's everyday lives and struggles, expressed through a wide range of institutions. In this instance politics is inextricably connected to pedagogies that effectively mobilize the beliefs, desires and forms of persuasion that organize and give meaning to particular strategies of social engagement and policy transformation. Education as a form of persuasion, power and intervention is constitutive of those ongoing struggles that shape the social. Challenging neo-liberal hegemony as a form of domination is crucial to reclaiming an alternative notion of the political and rearticulating the relationship between political agency and substantive democracy.[83]

Any viable notion of democracy should necessarily acknowledge the contradictions in the locution "democratic markets"—an expression which hides the fact that being a consumer is not tautonymous with being a citizen, and that unregulated free markets cannot produce democracy, social justice, a sustainable environment, and welfare for everybody.[84] A more honest account of what democracy means should be based on a notion of both individual and collective freedom that possesses self-limiting qualities. As Castoriadis so brilliantly suggests, "I can say that I am free in a society where there are laws, if I have had the effective possibility (and not only on paper) to participate in the discussion, deliberation, and formation of these laws. In other words, the legislative power should belong effectively to the collective, to the people."[85] In this way of thinking, freedom is understood as an activity and as a struggle. It is not given to us as a gift, it does not have a transparent meaning, and it needs to be redefined and struggled over. Freedom has its own rules, including the unique capacity to limit itself. Unlike what is happening in the capitalist societies that are unable to limit themselves and therefore become abusive to their citizens, freedom in a democracy sets its own limits. In a truly free and autonomous society, limits are put collectively to things that we can and cannot do. As Bauman suggests, "[t]he art of politics, if it happens to be democratic politics, is about dismantling the limits to citizens' freedom; but it is also about self-limitation: about making citizens free in order to enable them to set, individually and collectively, their own individual and collective limits."[86]

The recent collapse of the Argentinean economy attests to the absence of limits in the neoliberal order. It also attests to the detrimental results of twenty-six years of neoliberal economic policies under the guidance of International Monetary Fund. While the case of Argentina is an example par excellence of what happens when deregulated markets dictate the rules to the state, it also points to what people can do when they become aware of their civic power—which was strong enough in this case to over-turn a number of presidents and to push for a radical solution to the current economic and social impasse.

The case of Argentina also attests to Immanuel Wallerstein's assessment that world capitalism is actually in bad shape struc-turally, rather than enjoying a "new economy."[87] After five hun-dred years of existence, the world capitalist system is, for the first time, in true systemic crisis, and we find ourselves in an age of transition. Wallerstein does not think that the global offensive of capitalism and so-called globalization has strangled our possibil-ities. He believes that there is a spreading democratization of the world, evidenced by ever-expanding popular pressures for ex-penditures on health, education, and lifetime income guaran-tees, which have created a steady upward pressure of taxes as a share of world value created.

The 500,000 people who demonstrated in Barcelona against corporate Europe and neoliberal values are convinced that an-other world is possible. These activists rupture the inevitability and consensus of common sense because they understand free-dom in a different context: the freedom to oppose, the freedom to talk back, the freedom to dissent. The people demonstrating in Barcelona, Seattle, Washington, Genoa, and other parts of the world know that the market (dis)order is not inevitable, that there are alternatives, and that the language of critique and intervention can be part of a political project to oppose neolib-eralism—as was passionately suggested by Fidel Castro:

The market will dry up some day for the industry of lies; it is drying up already. If you really delve into the truth, you will realize that the political conception of imperialism, as well as the neoliberal economic order and globalization process im-posed on the world, is orphaned and defenseless when it comes to ideas and ethics. It is in this field that the main struggle of our times will be decided. And the final result of this battle, with no possible alternative, will be on the side of truth, and thus on the side of humanity.[88]

Education is the central arena in which humanity is going to be reinvented in our quest for decommodification and reclamation of the public sphere, and where a language that guarantees a political project for intervention will be cultivated. And this is where the need for a "counter-education" becomes a project for educators, cultural workers, artists, and activists. This type of counter-education, Castoriadis asserts, "call[s] for a new imaginary creation whose signification cannot be compared with anything similar in the past, a creation that would put at the center of human life significations other than the increase of production and consumption, that would set different goals that people would consider worth struggling for."[89] And Wallerstein claims, "[s]uch a world is possible. It is by no means certain that it will come into being. But then it is by no means impossible."[90]

NOTES

✥

Notes to Introduction

1. Paulo Freire, *The Politics of Education: Culture, Power, and Liberation* (Westport, CT: Bergin & Garvey, 1985), p. 103.

2. Ibid, p. 132.

3. James Crawford, "Obituary: The Bilingual Education Act, 1968–2002," *Rethinking Schools* 16, no.4 (Summer 2002), p. 1.

4. *The Boston Globe*, June 30, 2002.

5. Alan Lupo, "Accentuating the Negative," *The Boston Globe*, March 4, 1992, p. 19; "Humanities 101, Westfield style," *The Boston Globe*, March 3, 1992, p. 16.

6. Henry A. Giroux and Peter McLaren, "Teacher Education and the Politics of Engagement: The Case for Democratic Schooling," *Harvard Educational Review* 56, no. 3, (August 1986), pp. 213–238.

7. Mikhail Bakhtin, *The Dialogic Imagination*, trans. Caryl Emerson and Michael Holquist (Austin: University of Texas Press, 1981), p. 294.

8. Vaclav Havel, *Living in Truth* (London: Faber and Faber, 1989), p. 42.

9. Paulo Freire, *Pedagogy in Process* (New York: Seabury Press, 1978), pp. 13–14.

10. Ibid., p. 14.

11. Antonio Gramsci, *Selections from Prison Notebooks*, ed. and trans. Quinten Hoare and Geoffrrey Smith (New York: International Publishers, 1971), p. 52.

12. L. Rosenblatt, "The Enriching Values of Reading," in *Reading in the Age of Mass Communication*, ed. William S. Gray (New York: Appleton-Century Crofts, 1949).

13. Mell Gusson, "John Willet, Scholar and Translator of Brecht, Dies at 85," *New York Times*, August 24, 2002, p. A13.

14. Steven Erlanger, "At 100, Hitler's Filmmaker Sticks to Her Script," *New York Times*, August 24, 2002, p. A4.

15. Ibid., p. A4.

Notes to Chapter I

1. Donaldo Macedo and Lilia Bartolome, *Dancing With Bigotry: Beyond The Politics of Tolerance* (New York: St Martin's Press, 1999).

2. Norman Fairclough, *Critical Discourse Analysis: The Critical Study of Language* (New York: Addison Wesley Longman Inc., 1995), p. 7.

3. James Donald, "Language, Literacy and Schooling" in *The State and Popular Culture* (Milton Keynes: Open University Press, 1982), p. 32.

4. Fairclough, *Critical Discourse Analysis*, p. 7.

5. James Paul Gee, *Social Linguistics and Literacies: Ideology in Discourses* (Bristol, PA: Taylor & Francis, 1996), p. 131.

6. Jacques Derrida, *Positions* (Chicago: University of Chicago Press, 1981).

7. Ibid.

8. Pierre Bourdieu, *Language and Symbolic Power* (Cambridge, MA: Harvard University Press, 1991).

9. Donald "Language, Literacy and Schooling," p. 32.

10. Bourdieu, *Language and Symbolic Power*, p. 21.

11. Fairclough, *Critical Discourse Analysis*, p. 221.

12. According to Homi Bhabha, cultural diversity is understood as the recognitin of pre-given cultural contents and customs; held in a time-frame of relativism it gives rise to liberal notions of multiculturalism, cultural exchange or the culture of humanity. Homi Bhabha, "Staging the Politics of Difference: Homi Bhabha's Critical Literacy," in *Race, Rhetoric and the Postcolonial*, ed. by Gary A. Olson and

Lynn Worsham. (New York: State University of New York Press, 1999), p. 15.

13. Roland Barthes, *The Semiotic Challenge* (New York: Hill and Wang, 1988).

14. Bhabha, "Staging the Politics of Difference," p. 16.

15. Bourdieu, *Language and Symbolic Power.*

16. Ronald Wardaugh, *An Introduction to Sociolinguistics* (Oxford: Blackwell, 1998), p. 2.

17. Paulo Freire, *The Politics of Education: Culture, Power and Liberation* (New York: Bergin and Garvey, 1985).

18. For a more detailed discussion of black English, see J. L. Dillard, *Black English: Its History and Usage in the United States* (New York: Random House, 1972).

19. Fairclough, *Critical Discourse Analysis,* p. 94.

20. Donaldo Macedo, *Literacies of Power: What Americans Are Not Allowed to Know* (Boulder, CO: Westview Press, 1994), p. 45.

21. Albert Memmi, "*La Patrie Litteraire du Colonisé*," *Le Monde Diplomatique* (September 1996), p. 12.

22. Ngugi Wa' Thiongo, *Decolonizing the Mind: The Politics of Language in African Literature* (Portsmouth, NH: Heinemann, 1986).

23. Henry Giroux, *Fugitive cultures: Race, Violence and Youth* (New York: Routledge, 1996), p. 120.

24. Jurgen Habermas, *The Philosophical Discourse of Modernity: Twelve Lectures,* trans. F. Lawrence (Cambridge, MA: MIT Press, 1987).

25. Giroux, *Fugitive cultures,* p. 64.

26. Louis Althusser, *Essays on Ideology* (London: Verso, 1971), pp. 26, 30.

27. Ibid.

28. David Spener, "Transitional Bilingual Education and the Socialization of Immigrants" in *Breaking Free: The Transformative Power of Critical Pedagogy,* ed. Pepi Leistyna, Arlie Woodrum, and Stephen Sherblom (Cambridge: Harvard Educational Review, 1996).

29. Henry Giroux, *Theory and Resistance in Education: A Pedagogy for the Opposition* (South Hadley, MA: Bergin & Garvey, 1983), p. 235.

30. Antonia Darder, *Culture and Power in the Classroom: A Critical Foundation of Bicultural Education* (New York: Bergin and Garvey, 1991), p. 96.

31. bell hooks, *Teaching to Transgress: Education as the Practice of Freedom* (New York: Routledge, 1994), p. 168.

32. Ibid, p. 168.

33. Ibid, p. 168.

34. June Jordan quoted in hooks, *Teaching to Transgress*, p. 173.

Notes to Chapter II

1. This paper was delivered in 1998 at the Third International Conference of the Hellenic Association for the Study of English. It appeared in the Conference Proceedings: Eliza Kiti, ed., *The Other Within: Literature and Psychoanalysis, Linguistic and Cultural Theory* (Thessaloniki: Altintzis publishers, in press). It also appeared in: Bessie Dendrinos, *Language Education and Foreign Language Pedagogy: The Politics of ELT* (Athens: The University of Athens Publications, 2001).

2. Anastassios F. Christidis, *I Elliniki Glossa* [*The Greek Language*] (Ministry of Education and Religious Affairs, Division of International Educational Relations, Athens, 1996), pp. 13–17; David Graddol, *The Future of English?* (London: British Council, 1997).

3. Jacques Derrida, *Writing and Difference* (Chicago: Chicago University Press, 1978).

4. Cf. also Jacques Derrida, *Of Grammatology*, trans. G. Chakravorti Spivak (Baltimore: John Hopkins University Press, 1976).

5. E.g., E. M. Hatch, *Discourse and Language Education* (Cambridge: Cambridge University Press, 1992).

6. Michel Foucault, *The Archaeology of Knowledge* (London and New York: Routledge, 1972); Michel Foucault, *Power/Knowledge: Selected Interviews and Other Writings, 1972–1977*, ed. C. Gordon (New York: Pantheon Books, 1980); and Michel Foucault, "The Order of Discourse," in *Untying the Texts: A Post-Structuralist Reader*, ed. R. Young (London: Routlege and Kegan Paul, 1981).

7. cf. H. Fink-Eitel, *Foucault: An Introduction* (Philadelphia: Pennbridge Books, 1992), p. 38.

8. Foucault, *Power/Knowledge*, p. 244.

9. Pierre Bourdieu, *Language and Symbolic Power* (Cambridge, MA: Harvard University press, 1991), p. 45.

10. G. Williams, *Sociolinguistics: A Sociological Critique* (London and New York: Routledge, 1992), pp. 8–9.

11. Joshua Fishman, "Some Contrasts between Linguistically Homogeneous and Heterogeneous Polities," in *Language Problems of Developing Nations*, ed. Joshua A. Fishman, C. A. Ferguson, and L. Das Gupta (New York: Wiley, 1968), p. 60.

12. G. Williams, "Language Planning or Language Expropriation?" *Journal of Multilingual and Multicultural Development* 7, no. 6 (1986), p. 513.

13. Ibid.

14. Cf. Christos Lazos, "Litourgies tis glossas sto plaisio tou etnous-kratous" ["Functions of Language Within the Nation-State"]. Working Papers from the Conference "Strong and Weak Languages in the European Union: Aspects of Linguistic Hegemony" (Thessaloniki: Center for the Greek Language, 1996) pp. 61–77; Antonis Liakos, "Glossa kai Istoria sti Neoteri Ellada" ["Language and History in Modern Greece"], *The Greek Language* (Athens: Ministry of Education and Religious Affairs, Division of International Educational Relations, 1996), pp. 19–28; Anastasios F. Christidis, *Language, Politics, Culture* (Athens: Polis Publishers, 1999), p. 24.

15. J. McGowan, *Postmodernism and Its Critics* (Ithaca: Cornell University Press, 1991).

16. Derrida, *Of Grammatology*, p. 277.

17. R. Harris, *The Language Machine* (London: Duckworth, 1987).

18. Alastair Pennycook, *The Cultural Politics of English as an International Language* (London and New York: Longman, 1994), p. 117.

19. Ibid., pp. 126–129.

20. Dell Hymes, "Modes of the Interaction of Language and Social Life," in *Directions in Sociolinguistics: The Ethnography of Communication* ed. J. Gumperz and Dell Hymes (New York: Holt, Rinehart and Winston, 1972); M. Saville-Troike, *The Ethography of Communication: An Introduction*, Language in Society, 3 (Oxford: Blackwell, 1982).

21. S. Blum-Kulka and A. Olshtain, "Requests and apologies: A cross-cultural study of speech act realization patterns (CCSAPR)," *Applied Linguistics* 5 (1984), pp. 196–213; Maria Sifianou, *Politeness Phenomena in England and Greece: A Cross-Cultural Perspective* (Oxford: Clarendon Press, 1992); Deborah Tannen, "Cross-Cultural Communication," in *Handbook of Discourse Analysis 4: Discourse*

Analysis in Society, ed. Teun van Dijk (London: Academic Press, 1983).

22. See M. Cobarrubias, "Language planning: The State of the Art," in *Progress in Language Planning,* ed. M. Cobarrubias and Joshua Fishman (The Hague: Mouton, 1983).

23. Susan Sontag, "Elite Competition and Official Language Movements," and T. S. Donahue. "American Language Policy and Compensatory Opinion," in *Power and Inequality in Language Education,* ed. J. W. Tollefson (Cambridge: Cambridge University Press, 1995)..

24. cf. Henry A. Giroux, "Series Introduction: Literacy, Difference and the Politics of Border Crossing," in *Rewriting Literacy: Culture and the Discourse of the Other,* ed. Candace Mitchell and Kathryn Weiler (New York and London: Bergin and Garvey, 1991), p. xi.

25. John Fiske, *Reading the Popular* (Boston: Unwin Hyman, 1989), p. 149.

26. Michael Apple, *Education and Power* (Boston: Routledge and Kegan Paul, 1993), p. 9.

27. cf. Williams, *Sociolinguistics;* Robert Phillipson, *Linguistic Imperialism* (Oxford: Oxford University Press, 1992).

28. cf. B. B. Kachru, "The power and politics of English," *World Englishes* 5, no. 2/3 (1986), pp. 122, 135.

29. In virtually all of the European nations that are member states of the Union, linguistic hegemony has also prevailed within national boundaries. Language education and state language policies have by and large aimed at monoglossic and single discourse conditions. They have imposed the standard variety of the national language upon all social groups, including ethnic minorities that were often treated as potentially threatening unless they were assimilated into the dominant culture.

30. Robert Phillipson and Tove Skutnabb-Kangas, "English Only Worldwide or Language Ecology?" *TESOL Quarterly* 30, no. 3 (1996), pp. 429–52.

31. Of course pluri- or multilingualism, which is undoubtedly a precondition for democracy, should not be viewed as positive in itself, nor itself a value. It is positive attitudes to plurilingualism that should be aimed at, even though these too may be mythologized to the degree that structural conditions leading to economic exploitation may be ignored. For an interesting argument on the politics of multilingualist promotionism, see Christidis, Γλώσσα, Πολιτική, Πολιτισμός, pp. 154–65.

32. Gunther Kress, "Modes of Representation and Local Epistemologies: The Representation of Science in Education," (Unpublished paper, Institute of Education, University of London, 1998).

33. Derrida, *Of Grammatology*; Foucault, *Archaeology of Knowledge* and *Power/Knowledge*; Jacques Lacan, *Speech and Language in Psychoanalysis* (Baltimore: The John Hopkins University Press, 1968).

34. Ernesto Laclau and Chantal Mouffe, *Hegemony and Socialist Strategy* (London: Verso Books, 1985).

35. cf. Jina Politi, "Receptacles and Flows," in *The Other Within, Vol. 1*, ed. Ruth Parkin-Gounelas (Thessaloniki: A.A. Altintzis, 2001), pp. 9–23.

Notes to Chapter III

1. Gloria Anzaldúa, *Borderlands: The New Mestiza* (San Francisco: Aunt Lute, 1989).

2. Adam Pertam, "Buchanan Announces Presidential Candidacy," *Boston Globe*, Dec. 11, 1991, p. 1.

3. For a detailed description of the goals of U.S. English-only movement, see http://www.us-english.org/.

4. Mihailo Markovic, Liubomir Tadic, *Danko Grlik, Liberalismo y Socialismo: Teoria y Praxis* (Mexico:Editorial Grijalbo, 1977), p. 19.

5. Ibid., p. 17.

6. Geraldo Navas Davilla, *La Dialectica del Desarrollo Nacional: El Caso de Puerto Rico* (San Juan: Editorial Universitaria, 1978), p. 27.

7. Renato Constantino, *Neocolonial Identity and Counter-Consciousness* (London: Merlin Press, 1978), p. 66.

8. Ibid., p. 67.

9. Maria M. Lopez Lagunne, *Bilingualismo en Puerto Rico: Actitudes Sociolinguisticas del Maestro* (San Juan: M.I.S.C.E.S. Corp., 1989), p. 17.

10. Renato Constantino, *Neocolonial Identity and Counter-Consciousness* (London: Merlin Press, 1978), p. 66.

11. H. Eysenck, *The IQ Argument: Race, Intelligence, and Education* (New York: Library Press, 1971).

12. Arthur R. Jensen, "How Much Can We Boost IQ and Scholastic Achievement?" Harvard Educational Review 39 (1969), pp. 1–123.

13. Zeynep F. Beykont, "Academic Progress of a Nondominant Group: A Longitudinal Study of Puerto Ricans in New York City's Late Exit Bilingual Programs" (Doctoral Dissertation, Graduate School of Education, Harvard University, 1994); Virginia P. Collier, "A Synthesis of Studies Examining Long-Term Language Minority Student Data on Academic Achievement," *Bilingual Research Journal* 16 (1992), (182), pp. 187–212; James Cummins, "The Role of Primary Language Development in Promoting Educational Success for Language Minority Students" in *Schooling and Language Minority Students: A Theoretical Framework*, ed. California State Department of Education (Los Angeles: Evaluation, Dissemination and Assessment Center, California State University); Kenji Hakuta, *Mirror of Language: The Debate on Bilingualism* (New York: Basic Books, 1986).

14. Pepi Leistyna, *Presence of Mind: Education and Politics of Deception* (Boulder, CO: Westview Press, 1998).

15. Carry Nelson, *Manifesto of a Tenured Radical* (New York: New York University Press, 1997), p. 19.

16. Ibid., p. 19.

17. Henry A. Giroux, *Theory and Resistance: A Pedagogy for the Opposition* (South Hadley, MA: J.F. Bergin, 1983), p. 87.

18. Michael Schudson, *Discovering the News: A Social History of American Newspapers* (New York: Basic Books, 1978), p. 6.

19. Ibid., p. 6.

20. *San Diego Union Tribune*, "Bilingual Grads Outperform Others in Two Districts," July 8, 1998, p. 14.

21. For a comprehensive and critical discussion of scientific objectivity, see Donna Haraway, "Situated Knowledges: The Science Question in Feminism and the Privilege of Partial Perspectives," *Feminist Studies* 14 (1988), pp. 575–599.

22. Linda Brodkey, *Writing Permitted in Designated Areas Only* (Minnesota: Minnesota University Press, 1966), p. 10.

23. Ibid., p. 8.

24. Ibid., p. 8.

25. Roger Fowler et al., *Language and Control* (London: Routledge & Kegan Paul, 1979), p. 192.

26. Greg Myers, "Reality, Consensus, and Reform in the Rhetoric of Composition Teaching," *College English* 48, no. 2 (February 1986).

27. Jonathan Kozol, *Amazing Grace: The Lines and the Conscience of a Nation* (New York: Harper Perennial, 1996), p. 4.

28. Ibid., p. 39.

29. Richard J. Hernstein and Charles Murray, *The Bell Curve: Intelligence and Class Structure in American Life* (New York: The Free Press, 1994).

30. Kozol, *Amazing Grace,* p. 39.

31. Paulo Freire, *The Politics of Education: Culture, Power and Liberation* (Westport, CT: Bergin & Garvey, 1995), p. 103.

32. Gloria Anzaldúa, *Borderlands: The New Mestiza* (San Francisco: Spinsters/Aunt Lute, 1987), p. 203.

33. Ladislaus Semali and Joe L. Kincheloe, eds., *What is Indigenous Knowledge and Why Should We Study It?*

34. Joseph H. Suina, "And then I Went to School," in *Linguistic and Cultural Influences on Learning Mathematics,* ed. Rodney R. Cocking and Jose P. Mestre (Hillsdale, NJ: Lawrence Erlbaum Associates Publishers, 1998), p. 297.

35. Ngugi Wa' Thiongo, *Decolonizing the Mind: The Politics of Language in African Literature* (New Hampshire: Heinemann Press, 1986), p. 11.

36. Albert Memmi, *The Colonizer and the Colonized* (Boston: Beacon Press, 1967), p. 107.

37. Jean-Paul Sartre, "Introduction" to *The Colonizer and the Colonized,* by Albert Memmi (Boston: Beacon Press, 1967), pp. xxiv-xxv.

38. Amilcar Cabral, *Return to the Source* (New York and London: Monthly Review Press, 1974), p. 16.

39. Catherine E. Snow, M. Susan Burns, and Peg Griffin, eds., *Committee on the Prevention of Reading Difficulties in Young Children* (Washington, DC: 1998), p. 29.

40. Ibid., pp. 27–28.

41. Celia T. Leyva, "Language Philosophy Research Paper," presented to a graduate class in sociolinguistics, University of Massachusetts, Boston, Fall, 1998.

42. bell hooks, *Teaching to Transgress* (New York: Routledge, 1996), p. 168.

43. Ibid., p. 168.

44. Saul Levine, "On Guns and Health Care, the U.S. Caves in to Force," *San Diego Union Tribune,* Aug. 12, 1993, p. 11.

45. Paulo Freire, *The Politics of Education: Culture, Power and Liberation* (New York: Bergin and Garvey Publishers, 1985), p. 57.

Notes to Chapter IV

1. An earlier version of this paper was presented at the International Conference on Discourse and Racism: An Issue for Critical Discourse Analysis, held at the Institut für Sprachwissenschaft Angewandte Sprachwissenschaft of the University of Vienna, in May 1998. The paper in its present form appears in *The Semiotics of Racism: Approaches in Critical Discourse Analysis* by Martin Reisigl and Ruth Wodak (Vienna: Passagen-Verlag, 2000). It has also appeared in *Language Education and Foreign Language Pegagogy: The Politics of ELT* by Bessie Dendrinos (Athens: The University of Athens publications, 2001).

2. Ben Agger, *The Discourse of Domination: From the Frankfurt School to Postmodernism* (Evanston, IL: Northwestern University Press, 1992).

3. See, for example, Teun van Dijk, "Political Discourse and Racism: Describing Others in Western Parliaments," Ruth Wodak, "Das Ausland and Anti-Semitic Discourse: The Discursive Construction of the Other," and Michael Hoechsmann, "Bennetton Culture: Marketing the Difference to the New Global Consumer," in *The Language and Politics of Exclusion*, ed, Stephen Harold Riggins. (Thousand Oaks, London, New Delhi: Sage Publications, 1997).

4. Phillipson, "Linguicism," p. 339. Phillipson's and Kangas's views on linguicism are based on the notion of linguicist ideology, as discussed by Roy Preiswerk, ed., *The Slant of the Pen: Racism in Children's Books* (Geneva: World Council of Churches, 1980).

5. Jana Sawicki, "Identity Politics and Sexual Freedom: Foucault and Feminism," in *Feminism and Foucault: Reflections on Resistance*, ed. I. Diamond and L. Quinby (Boston: Northwestern University, 1998), p. 185.

6. E.g., George W. Beadle, "The New Biology and the Nature of Man," in *Norton Reader: An Anthology of Expository Prose*, ed. Arthur M. Eastman (New York: W.W. Norton & Co., 1969), pp. 1294–95); William R. Schultz, *Genetic Codes of Culture? The Deconstruction of Tradition by Kuhn, Bloom and Derrida* (New York and London: Garland Publishing, 1994).

7. Wodak agrees with Guillaumin (1991) whom she quotes, say-

ing that "the term 'race' lacks semantic boundaries." See Wodak, *Das Ausland and anti-semitic discourse*, p. 70; C. Guillaumin, "Rasse, das Wort und die Vorstellung," in *Das Eigene und das Fremde: Neur Rassismus in der alten Welt?* ed. U. Bielefeld (Hamburg, Germany: Junius, 1991), pp. 65–90.

8. Michel Foucault, *The Archaeology of Knowledge* (London and New York: Routledge, 1972), and *Power/Knowledge: Selected Interviews and Other Writings, 1972–1977*, ed. C. Gordon (New York: Pantheon Books, 1980).

9. Cf. Joshua Fishman, "Language Ethnicity and Racism," in *Sociolinguistics*, ed. N. Coupland and A. Jaworski (New York: St. Martin's Press, 1997); van Dijk, "Political Discourse," p. 32.

10. This project is part of a large-scale study coordinated by a group of scholars from the University of Crete, Department of Primary Education, Centre of Intercultural and Immigration Studies, directed by Professor M. Damanakis. (See http://www.cc.ucr.gr/diaspora.) It is carried out in the framework of a program funded by the European Union under the auspices of the Greek Ministry of National Education and Religion: "Πρόλραμμα Παιδείας Ομολενών."

11. Lachman M. Khubchandani, "Philosophical Issues of Contact Language Planning" in *"Strong" and "Weak" Languages in the European Union: Aspects of Linguistic Hegemonism, Vol. I*, ed. Anastasios F. Christidis (Thessaloniki: Centre for the Greek Language, 1997), pp. 43–49.

12. Norman Fairclough, *Language and Power* (London and New York: Longman, 1989), p. 22.

13. James Tollefson, *Planning Language, Planning Inequality* (London and New York: Longman, 1991), p. 208.

14. Joshua Fishman, "Some contrasts between linguistically homogeneous and heterogeneous polities," in *Language Problems of Developing Nations*, ed. J. A. Fishman, C. A Ferguson and L. Das Gupta (New York: Wiley, 1968), p. 60.

15. Glyn Williams, "Language Planning or Language Expropriation?" *Journal of Multilingual and Multicultural Development 7*, no. 6 (1986), p. 513.

16. Alastair Pennycook, *The Cultural Politics of English as an International Language* (London and New York: Longman, 1994), p. 117.

17. S. Blum-Kulka and A. Olshtain, "Requests and apologies: A

cross-cultural study of speech act realization patterns (CCSAPR)," *Applied Linguistics* 5 (1984), pp. 196–213; Maria Sifianou, *Politeness Phenomena in England and Greece: A Cross-Cultural Perspective* (Oxford: Clarendon Press, 1992); Deborah Tannen, "Cross-Cultural Communication," in *Handbook of Discourse Analysis 4: Discourse Analysis in Society*, ed. Teun van Dijk (London: Academic Press, 1983).

18. Emanuel Schegloff, "The Routine as Achievement," *Human Studies* 9 (1986), pp. 111–51.

19. Robert Hopper, *Telephone Conversations* (Bloomington: Indiana University Press, 1992).

20. M. Syer, "Racism, Ways of Thinking and School," and C. Mullard, "Multilingual Education in Britain: From Assimilation to Cultural Pluralism," in *Race, Migration and Schooling*, ed. J. Tierney (London: Holt Education, 1982).

21. *Dossier for the Education Information Network for the European Union: The Education System in the Federal Republic of Germany* (Secretariat of the Standing Conference of the Ministers of Education and Cultural Affairs of the Länder in the Federal Republic of Germany, 1995), Section 5, Secondary Education, sub-section 5.3.2.12, "Support programmes for foreign children," pp. 120–21.

22. See "Information of the 1994 Curriculum for the Compulsory School System LPO 94" (Stockholm: Swedish Ministry of Education and Science, 1996) and the *EURYDICE* document, "The Swedish Education System," (Stockholm: Swedish Ministry of Education and Science, 1996).

23. J. L. Clark, *Curriculum Renewal in School Foreign Language Learning* (Oxford: Oxford University Press, 1987), p. 91.

24. Ibid, pp. 91–92

25. It should be noted that the language education offered in British state schools is quite different from the language education addressed specifically to Greek minority children in Greek community schools, which operate in various parts of Britain. In this case, Modern Greek is offered as a foreign language for anyone who wishes to study it. Yet, statistics show that few schools offer it, supposedly on account of the conclusion that few children who are not of Greek descent would choose to study it.

26. See *Modern Languages in the National Curriculum*, a document published in 1991 by the British Department of Education and Science, and the Welsh Office, HMSO.

27. Tuku Mukherjee, "ESL: An Imported New Empire?" *Journal of Moral Education* 15, no. 1 (1986), pp. 43–50.

28. See, for example, G. Ypsilandis, "Contrastive Pragmatics in Language Teaching and Learning." Paper delivered at the Third International Conference of HASE: The Other Within in Thessaloniki, Greece at the School Of English, Aristotle University of Thessaloniki, 1998.

29. Jacques Derrida, *Of Grammatology*, trans. G. Chakravorti Spivak (Baltimore: John Hopkins University Press, 1976); Jacques Lacan, *Speech and Language in Psychoanalysis* (Baltimore: The John Hopkins University Press, 1968); Ernesto Laclau and Chantal Mouffe, *Hegemony and Socialist Strategy* (London: Verso Books, 1985).

Notes to Chapter V

This paper is part of Panayota Gounari's doctoral dissertation to be submitted to the College of Education (Department of Curriculum and Instruction) at Pennsylvania State University.

1. Zygmunt Bauman, *In Search of Politics* (Stanford, CA: Stanford University Press, 1999), p. 8.

2. For a more detailed discussion, see Henry Giroux, "Something is Missing: From Utopianism to a Politics of Educated Hope," in *Public Spaces, Private Lives: Beyond the Culture of Cynicism* (Boulder, CO: Rowman & Littlefield, 2001). For works of "neo-liberal utopianism," see Francis Fukuyama, *The End of History and the Last Man (Avon Books, 1993)* and Dinesh D'Souza, *The End of Racism: Principles for a Multiracial Society* (Touchstone Books, 1996), among others.

3. Cornelius Castoriadis, *The Rise of Insignificance* (Athens, Greece: Ypsilon Books, 2000), p. 122.

4. Ibid, p. 122.

5. Carl Boggs, *The End of Politics* (New York: Guilford Press, 2000).

6. Herbert Marcuse, *One-Dimensional Man* (Boston: Beacon Press, 1964), p. 85.

7. Bauman, *In Search of Politics*, p. 127.

8. Marcuse, *One-Dimensional Man*, p. 87.

9. Susan George, "A Short History of Neo-liberalism: Twenty Years of Elite Economics and Emerging Opportunities for Structural Change" in *ZMagazine* (http://www.zmag.org/CrissesCurEvts/Globalism/george.htm) March 1999.

10. Lawrence Grossberg quoted in *Impure Acts: The Practical Politics of Cultural Studies* by Henry Giroux (New York: Routledge, 2000), p. 10.

11. Zsuzsa Ferge, "What are the State Functions that Neoliberalism Wants to Eliminate?" in *Not for Sale: In Defense of Public Goods*, ed. Anatole Anton, Milton Fisk, and Nancy Holmstrom (Boulder, CO: Westview Press, 2000), p. 182.

12. Ulrich Beck, "Redefining Power in the Global Age: Eight Theses," *Dissent* (Fall 2001), p. 86.

13. Karl Polanyi, *The Great Transformation: The Political and Economic Origins of our Time* (Boston: Beacon Press, 1957 [1944]), p. 73.

14. Cornelius Castoriadis, "Contre le Conformisme Generalisé: Stopper la Montée de l'Insignificance," *Le Monde Diplomatique* (August 1998), pp. 22–23.

15. Giroux, *Public Spaces, Private Lives*, p. 118.

16. Ibid.

17. Colin Leys, *Market Driven Politics: Neoliberal Democracy and the Public Interest* (London: Verso, 2001), p. 3.

18. Holy Sklar, *Imagine a Country* in *Znet CrossCurrents* (July 1997).

19. For a more detailed discussion, see Barbara Ehrenreich, *Nickel and Dimed: On (Not) Getting By in America* (New York: Metropolitan Books, 2001).

20. "Strike Leaving Shelves, Snackers' Wants Unfilled," *Boston Globe*, March 20, 2000, Section A1.

21. Pierre Bourdieu, *Acts of Resistance: Against the Tyranny of the Market* (New York: The New Press), p. 96.

22. Ferge, "What are the State Functions Neoliberalism Wants to Eliminate?" p. 182.

23. Ulrich Beck, "Redefining Power in the Global Age: Eight Theses," *Dissent* (Fall 2001), p. 86.

24. Bourdieu, *Acts of Resistance*, p. 32.

25. Beck, "Redefining Power in the Global Age," p. 83.

26. Bauman, *In Search of Politics*, p. 74.

27. Beck, "Redefining Power in the Global Age," p. 83.

28. Bauman, *In Search of Politics*, pp. 127–128.

29. Terry Eagleton, *Ideology: An Introduction* (London: Verso Books, 1991), pp. 28–30.

30. Susan George, "A Short History of Neo-liberalism," on ZNet, *http://www.zmag.org/CrisesCurEvts/Globalism/george.htm*, (1999).

31. Ibid.

32. Milton and Rose Friedman, *Free to Choose: A Personal Statement* (San Diego: Harcourt Brace, 1980), p. 390.

33. Bourdieu, *Acts Of Resistance,* p. 50.

34. Giroux, *Public Spaces, Private Lives,* p. 56.

35. Bourdieu, *Acts Of Resistance,* p. 29.

36. Marcuse, *One-Dimensional Man,* p. 87–88.

37. Ibid, p. 94.

38. Benjamin Barber, "Blood Brothers, Consumers, or Citizens? Three Models of Identity—Ethnic, Commercial, and Civic," in *Cultural Identity and the Nation State,* ed. Carol Gould and Pasquale Pasquino (Lanham: Rowman & Littlefield, 2001), p. 59.

39. Marcuse, *One-Dimensional Man,* pp. 7–8.

40. Derek Bok, *The Cost of Talent: How Executives and Professionals Are Paid and How It Affects America* (New York: The Free Press, 1993), p. 260.

41. Bauman, *In Search of Politics,* p. 4.

42. Friedman, *Free to Choose,* p. 65.

43. Robert Reich, *The Future of Success* (New York: Alfred A Knopf, 2001), p. 217.

44. Jeff Gates, "Modern Fashion or Global Fascism?" *Tikkun* 17, no. 1 (2002), pp. 30–31.

45. Bauman, *In Search of Politics,* pp. 72–73.

46. Data retrieved from *www.inequality.org.*

47. Annamaria Lusardi, "Increasing Saving Among the Poor: The Role of Financial Literacy," *Joint Center for Poverty Research Newsletter* 6, no. 1 (Jan.-Feb. 2002).

48. Ibid.

49. *Fortune* (Sept. 4, 2000) cited in www.inequality.org by Chris Hartman.

50. Grossman cited in Giroux, *Impure Acts,* p. 101.

51. For a more detailed discussion, see Ehrenreich, *Nickel and Dimed.*

52. Ehrenreich, *Nickel and Dimed,* p. 26.

53. Ibid, pp. 25–26.

54. Paul Street, "The Economy is Doing Fine, It's Just the People that Aren't" in ZNet *Domestic Policy http://www.zmag.org/ZMag/articles* (November 2000).

55. Ibid.

56. Barber, "Blood Brothers, Consumers, or Citizens?" p. 59.

57. Bok, *The Cost of Talent*, p. 258.

58. Giroux, p. 133.

59. Anatole Anton, "Public Goods as Commonstock: Notes on the Reading Commons," in *Not for Sale: In Defence of Public Goods*, ed. Anatole Anton, Milton Fisk, and Nancy Holmstrom (Boulder, CO: Westview Press, 2000), p. 11.

60. Gates, "Modern Fashion or Global Fascism?"

61. Paul Street, "Free to Be Poor: The 'Devil's Gift' at Millenium's Turn" in *Znet* (June 2001).

62. Statistics retrieved from Sklar, *Imagine a Country*.

63. Friedman, *Free to Choose*, p. 66.

64. Bauman, *In Search of Politics*, p. 78.

65. Max Horkheimer, *Critique of Pure Reason* (New York: Seabury, 1974), p. 139.

66. Edward Said, "Thoughts About America," *Al-Ahram Weekly* (March 2, 2002).

67. Hanah Arendt, *Origins of Totalitarianism* (New York: Harvest Books, 1973), p. 466.

68. Ibid, p. 466.

69. Henry Giroux, *The Mouse that Roared: Disney and the End of Innocence* (Boulder, CO: Rowman & Littlefield, 1999), p. 3.

70. Friedman, *Free to Choose*, p. 177.

71. Ibid, p. 177.

72. Anton, *Public Goods as Commonstock*, p. 2.

73. Boggs, *The End of Politics*, p. 11.

74. Henry Giroux, *Pedagogy and the Politics of Hope: Theory, Culture and Schooling* (Boulder, CO: Westview Press, 1997), p. 236.

75. Street, "The Economy is Doing Fine, It's Just the People That Aren't," *ZNet* (November 2000).

76. Zygmunt Bauman *In Search of Politics* (Stanford, CA: Stanford University Press, 1999).

77. Barber, p. 59.

78. Giroux, p. 53.

79. Hommi Bhabha, *Staging the Politics of Difference: Homi Bhabha's Critical Literacy* in *Race, Rhetoric and the Postcolonial*, ed. Gary A. Olson and Lynn Worsham (New York: State University of New York Press, 1999), pp. 3–39.

80. Bhabha, Ibid, p. 29.

81. Cornelius Castoriadis, *Philosophy, Politics, Autonomy*, ed. David Ames Curtis (New York: Oxford University Press, 1991), p. 77.

82. Ibid.
83. Giroux, *Public Spaces, Private Lives,* p. 53.
84. Barber, "Blood Brothers, Consumers, or Citizens?" p. 59.
85. Cornelius Castoriadis, "De l'Autonomie en Politique," *Le Monde Diplomatique* (February 1998), p. 23.
86. Bauman, *In Search of Politics,* p. 4.
87. Immanuel Wallerstein, "A Left Politics for an Age of Transition," *Monthly Review* 53, no. 8 (January 2002), p. 18.
88. Fidel Castro, "Cuba will Neither Negotiate nor Sell out its Revolution, Which has Cost the Blood and Sacrifice of Many of its Sons and Daughters." Interview with Federico Mayor Zaragoza in *Intercambio* (June 2000).
89. Castoriadis, *The Rise of Insignificance,* p. 129.
90. Wallerstein, "A Left Politics for an Age of Transition," p. 23.

About the Authors

Donaldo Macedo is Distinguished Professor of Liberal Arts and Education at University of Massachusetts, Boston. He is a leading authority in language education and has published many books and articles in the areas of applied linguistics and critical literacy. For many years he was a coauthor with and translator of the late Paulo Freire. He is collaborator with Noam Chomsky on the recently published book, *Chomsky on Miseducation*.

Bessie Dendrinos is Professor of Sociology of Language and Foreign Language Education at the National and Kapodistrian University of Athens. Concerned with language politics and language-education policies, particularly in Europe, she is well known for her critical analysis of the discursive practices of English language teaching and foreign language pedagogies.

Panayota Gounari is Assistant Professor in the Applied Linguistics Graduate Program at the University of Massachusetts, Boston. Her primary areas of interest include language policy, the analysis of language in its relation to social change, and hegemony and the implications for democracy and human agency.

INDEX

෴

Index

Index

Index

Index

adoption of solely a surveillance
role, 120
intervention, minimal, demand
for 120
strategy, "operational," 125–126
as threat to democracy, 111
voting, 138
wealth,
polarization of, 128
implies an illusory choice, 138
parallels with shopping, 132
Non-English speakers, 10

Oakland, California, 28
Objectivity,
erroneous nature of the claim to
"scientific," 71
scientific, 76
Othering, 89
"Otherness," 12

Patriarchy, 39
Patriot Act, 134, 135
Pedagogy, critical, 24
Pennycook, Alastair, 51
Philippines, United States educational
policy in, 66–67
Phillipson, Robert, 90
Pluralism/culturalism, 95
Polanyi, Karl, 113–114
Politics, market-driven, 114–115
Positivism, 3, 4, 17, 20, 51, 58
and rationality, triumph of, in
neoliberal discourse, 112
excess of, 85
method of enquiry, 70
Power relations, theory, 14
Prejudices, language-related, 89
Pseudoscientists, (see scientists, -
pseudo)
Public spending, 62
Puerto Rico, United States
educational policy in, 67

Race, class, and gender, 3–5
struggles, 89
Racial identity, 91
Racism, 39,

cultural, 91
hierarchical, 92
ideological elements that generate
and sustain the cruel reality
of, 72
linguistic, 11, 12
Rationality, 50
Reich, Robert, 128
Riefenstahl, Leni, 19

Said, Edward, 134–35
Sartre, Jean Paul, 83
Saussure, Ferdinand de,
approaches to language, 31–32
conception of *la langue* and
idealization of the nation
state, 51
Savings and Loan scandal, 62
Schools,
as sites for struggle and
contestation, 40
as sites where legitimate knowledge
and language are reproduced,
41
colonial, 15
Schudson, Michael, 70
Science, 3
as a license for dehumanization, 67
hard, call for in the social sciences,
69
need for self-criticism, skepticism
and contestation in, 76
Scientism, 70
Scientists, -pseudo, 69–72, 76
Skutnabb-Kangas, Tove, 90
Society, 100
Sociolinguistics, 51, 96
Sociolinguistics, treated as hard
science, 3
Sontag, Susan, 53
Spanish,
as a language of instruction, 9
language, 9
Specialization, academic, 2
Speech, comparative and contrastive
studies of, 52, 96–97
Street, Paul, 131–132
Structuralism, 51

Index

Students,
  bilingual, democratic rights of, 83
  educational programs for, 82
  linguistic minority, 87
Suina, Joseph H., 79
Sweden, opportunities for children to
    receive education in their
    "first" language, 98
Syer, M., 97

Tadic, Liubomir, 65
Tavera, T.H. Pardo de, 66
Technicism, pure, problems with, 77
TESOL, 10
Thiongo, Ngugi Wa', 37, 79
Title VII, 7
Tollefson, James, 96
Twinkies, (see Interstate Bakery
    Corp, coverage of strike at)
United States,
  colonial
    legacy of, 66
    model of education, 41
    values, inculcation of, 67
  corporations, major, 136
  doctrinal system, 41
  educational
    policy, 41

institutions, changing nature of,
    136
foreign policy, dominant discourse
    of, 115
healthcare system, 135
higher education
  curriculum, subordination to
    corporate needs, 136
  exploitation of GAs and TAs,
    136
  language policy of, 34–35
  media, 135–136
  prisons, corporate privatization of,
    136–137
  public arena, degeneration of, 137

Unz, Ron, 6

Van Dijk, Teun, 92

Wallerstein, Immanuel, 143
Wardaugh, Ronald, 33
Wealth, (see Neoliberalism, wealth)
Western heritage, primacy of, versus
    multiculturalism, 80
Willett, John, 18
Williams, G., 49